Extraordinary Christianity

Extraordinary Christianity

The Life and Thought of Alexander Vinet

by PAUL T. FUHRMANN

with a Preface by JOHN T. McNEILL

THE WESTMINSTER PRESS

Philadelphia

LIBRARY OF CONGRESS CATALOG CARD No. 64–10520

PUBLISHED BY THE WESTMINSTER PRESS®

PHILADELPHIA, PENNSYLVANIA 19107

PRINTED IN THE UNITED STATES OF AMERICA

In this world things fade and fall off
Once they have passed their season
But in the Kingdom of Christ
The new man is vigorous and flour-
ishes;
To this alone we must pay attention.

—*John Calvin*

Our doctrine is the teaching of love:
the compassionate love of God;
the grateful love of man.

—*A. Vinet*

Contents

Preface

It has been my privilege to read the manuscript of this book, and I am now permitted to say a word in commendation of the printed volume. For half a lifetime Professor Fuhrmann has given thoughtful attention to the work of Alexander Vinet, and nobody is in a better position to be the interpreter of the eminent Swiss thinker. Vinet's numerous writings on religious subjects and on aspects of French literature won, chiefly after his death, a wide international circulation, many of them appearing repeatedly in English editions. In all this literary production, as well as in decisive actions of his career, he revealed a notable combination of spirituality, sagacity, and love of liberty. His *Pastoral Theology* and *Homiletics* were long highly esteemed in theological schools, and although they are unfortunately no longer familiar, their quality is hardly surpassed in any age by writers on the tasks of the ministry. His books of this class, however, present only one aspect of a comprehensive body of thought, searching, evangelical, and free, that deserves renewed attention amid the theological concerns of our time. He was no mere continuator or retailer of other men's ideas. Søren Kierkegaard refers to Vinet's previous affirmation of one of his own chief contentions, with the remark, "Vinet says it in masterly fashion." This may well remind us of the place taken by Vinet both as a pioneering theologian and as an unusually gifted writer. His was the lofty spirit of the great thinkers of the Christian ages, and he surpasses most theologians both in clarity and in charity. His style has such freshness and originality that his work never goes stale. After long neglect his mind speaks out of this book with utterance to command attention. That which Vinet, more than anyone, did for Pascal is here deservedly done for Vinet himself. In this admirable book Dr. Fuhrmann will gladden old acquaintances of Vinet and win for him a host of new admirers.

JOHN T. McNEILL

Introduction

I first became acquainted with Vinet in 1920 for the simple reason that he has always been a great spiritual force among French-speaking Protestants. From 1922 to 1935 the Christianity of Vinet and Pascal dominated my thinking. Between 1930 and 1933 I had occasion to write down the substance of about three chapters of this book. About the year 1935 I had a turning point in my life, that is, I became vitally interested in Calvin. But nothing in Calvin indicated that I should let Vinet go his way. On the contrary, I found that Vinet happily complemented Calvin. Calvin, who died in 1564, evidently could not examine from a Christian point of view the later literatures of various nations or give a Christian estimate of our modern culture and civilization, while Vinet does all this for us.

It would be ingratitude to omit bringing in a few names here. The late Dr. William Rodemann of Knoxville College encouraged me to write an article about Vinet which, thanks to him, was published in *The Lutheran Church Quarterly* of July, 1946. Professor Rodemann taught that a philosophy of religion ought to complement Reformation thought. He and I certainly agreed that just to believe what everybody believes and to do what everybody does is mere nativism—not Christianity. Dr. Rodemann cultivated Vinet as well as Berdyaev and Soloviëv. These authors raise their readers above their environments, ennoble life for them, and free them from several evils. Vinet was a man of letters, a journalist, a preacher, a poet, a philosopher—and a Christian. His complete and universal thought meets the needs of all nations and all denominations. Vinet's spirituality keeps his readers from being suffocated by society and dying intellectually.

In 1946 I first made the acquaintance of Dr. John T. McNeill. This great scholar has ever since taken an interest in my studies, including that of Vinet, whose work was already highly regarded by Dr. McNeill.

At this juncture I must also mention the name of Noel Christol, whom I came to know by chance on a Paris boulevard. I had mistaken him for one of the professors of the Protestant School of Theology. He was at that time the Protestant chaplain of La Santé prison. Those of my readers who have seen the French play and movie *It Is Midnight, Dr. Schweitzer!* will recall that when Albert Schweitzer first went to Africa, his missionary post was occupied by Noel Christol, and it was Christol who, with strong philosophical quotations, kept Dr. Schweitzer from despair. "Where did you find such masterly thoughts?" asked Schweitzer. "In the books of Dr. Schweitzer!" answered Christol. From this extraordinary man, Noel Christol, I got the idea of reading my own manuscript for my own spiritual upbuilding, and several times these pages saved me from discouragement. The manuscript was read by others and was found to be a source of inspiration to them.

These pages of introduction are designed to meet beforehand some questions that my readers may raise.

"Why," it will be asked, "did you write this book about Vinet?" I will answer: simply for personal gratification, that is, for the enrichment of my own life and that of the persons who showed some interest in this man Vinet, who at the age of twenty was made professor of French literature in Basel, 1817, and often preached in the French Reformed Church of that city. As Senator Schérer said: "Vinet ascended the pulpit because he had something to say. His hearers felt that he was true to himself and that what he offered was his very life."

A second question is asked: "To whom is this book addressed?" It is directed to the average man and woman who, finding local preaching inadequate or irrelevant, longs for something different. It is quite possible that such persons may find in these pages the type of Christianity that they unconsciously seek. There is no doubt that Vinet intellectually goes deeper and higher than our constituencies permit our preachers to go. The Bible is the infallible rule of faith and morals, but who ever raises the problem of the quality of the minds of those who read the Bible? How many persons, after all, do realize that between the infallible Bible and our own self there is our mind? And that that mind has been conditioned by our environment, race, parentage, and education? A mind will see in the Bible only what that mind is able to perceive. A mean man will read the Bible with a mean mind. A vulgar fellow will justify his immense ignorance with quotations from the Bible, while a noble man will see noble things in that same Bible. And such a noble man was certainly Vinet. He had a great mind and saw great things in the Bible, which without the Spirit remains a dead letter.

Since Vinet later in life taught homiletics and pastoral theology, this book naturally ought to be useful to ministers of the gospel. He offers innumerable gems—thoughts that can be easily inserted in discourses or expanded into sermons. Vinet offers not only substance but form as well. Many of his suggestions for preaching and pastoral care may prove to be valuable to pastors.

Another audience of Vinet is composed of theological students, professors, and intellectuals who may be tired of current ideas—be these orthodox, unorthodox, or neoorthodox. These persons will find something new in these pages. As Vinet offers a complete Christian thought on all the various aspects of human life, he could open new horizons and offer numerous subjects for research, themes for students' essays, and topics for doctoral dissertations.

I have above partly answered a third question, which is: "How might this book be put to best use?" Professors, Sunday school teachers, and students of theology may find that Vinet corrects today's excessive objectivism in theology. He makes man accept the truth that is outside and beyond man by starting and first resting on truths found in man. How many theologues, after all, realize that today the great problem is not God but man? It is man who is in bad shape and in need of restoration. Vinet is concerned about humanity. He does not accept man's degradation but wants to meet him on a higher level. Vinet makes religion cease to be an ensemble of external doctrines and commandments. He makes Christianity become a new life in us that transforms everything it touches. Vinet was not a professional and technical theologian in the narrow sense of this word. Rather, he represented the spirit of Christianity. Vinet presented many of its still unknown aspects, put to light its capital truths for us moderns, and opened a new vista on the spiritual progress of society and church.

Men and women interested in ecumenicity will appreciate Vinet. He was born in and grew in the Reformed Protestant tradition, but he fully realized its limitations. Vinet was not hostile to Catholics. As a matter of fact, one of his cherished dreams was to write a life and history of Francis of Sales, 1567–1622. He thought indeed that the Protestants' emphasis on mere faith was sterile. According to Vinet, faith saves because it creates hope and charity. He no doubt would have loved to quote these words of Francis of Sales: "Just as the queen of bees never goes to the fields without being accompanied by her whole little people, so charity never enters a heart without lodging therein the whole train of all other virtues. . . . Love holds the first rank among the passions of the soul: love is the king of all movements of the heart; it converts all else to itself and makes us that which it loves, Hos. 9:10."

The great literary critic Sainte-Beuve found that what was most striking in Vinet was "a spirit of light and infinite Christian charity." Forgiveness and acceptance do not constitute the whole of Christianity. They are not enough. Vinet leads on. He never tired of repeating, "Conversion is only sanctification begun, and sanctification is only conversion continued." We shall be saved

by grace, or we shall not be saved at all. But it is equally certain
for Vinet that without holiness none shall see the Lord; and
it must needs be that the sanctification of one's heart should
have for its effect the sanctification of one's conduct. The second
reproduces the first, as a statue reproduces the curves of the
mold in which it is cast; and it is in this sense that the gospel,
as well as the law, can say that everyone, in the Day of Judgment, shall receive "according to the deeds done in the body,
whether they be good or whether they be evil." And he noted
that if Jesus Christ, as deliverer, enters at once into a person,
Jesus Christ, as love and the true new man, grows therein slowly
and laboriously. Vinet insisted that the unloving is not a Christian and that Christianity aims at leading us to love. Science
and knowledge can give us convictions, love alone can give us
life. Vinet tells us that we must not make any mistake here.
The equally gentle and majestic image or idea of a good God
does not naturally belong to the thought and imagination of
man. It is only the gospel that has disclosed it to our mind: a
loving God is a revealed God.

A fourth question will be asked: "Why has this book no
notes?" The reason is that the editors were horrified at the number of references, footnotes, and foreign books indicated in the
original manuscript. If my notes and my list of Vinet's works
and of the books about him in French, German, Italian, and
Spanish had been printed here, the price of this book would
have been prohibitive. The editors also noted that the biblio-
graphical references in the original typescript were almost all
unavailable to our readers. It seemed unfair to ask them to pay
for having this material in the book. The editors and I agreed
therefore to omit the original list of foreign works consulted,
all the notes, and innumerable references to Vinet's works and
studies of his thought. If a student wants to pursue a study of
Vinet or an aspect of his thought, if a reader desires to verify
my statements, a copy of the original typescript has been de-
posited in the libraries of Columbia Theological Seminary in
Decatur, Georgia, of Union Theological Seminary in New York

City, and of the School of Theology of the University of Geneva. The text, references, list of all the works I have used, and the notes of my original manuscript can therefore be consulted in these libraries. If the reader considers that I took several trips to Europe to gather materials and ideas for this book, it is not too much to ask those readers and students who want to pursue this study of Vinet to write to or go to the libraries of the divinity schools mentioned above.

I hope others will share my conviction that a knowledge of Vinet's thought has value and importance for contemporary readers. The reasons that I may add to my previous considerations are mainly two, one negative and one positive. And I state them in the words of Vinet.

Man lives not by bread alone. He cannot live any more on glory and liberty. Other needs more profound, more vast, agitate him. Man unconsciously thirsts for God and things eternal. Civilization and science do not change the groundwork of our nature; they may indeed divert some persons from the feeling of these wants, but amid all degrees of civilization, and in all forms of social life, man is a pilgrim and a stranger upon earth.

Vinet quoted Pascal's saying that "rivers are highways that march forward, and carry us whither we would go, nay, even whither we would not go." And what Vinet said in this connection I may well apply to Vinet himself. Vinet is like a great river of ideas and sentiments that will transport our reader where he wants to go and even where the reader does not want to go. Vinet does not content himself with tracing by his words an immovable road through life. He animates the way, gives meaning to it. He makes the road before us to become movement, life, and strength. He opens out in our persons the source of a new life and the treasure of a perfect light that no false glimmer will ever be able to replace.

PAUL T. FUHRMANN

Extraordinary Christianity

I

The Life and Death
of Alexander Vinet

A LEXANDER VINET, the greatest French-speaking Protestant thinker since Calvin, was born at Ouchy near Lausanne on June 17, 1797.

The Vinet family originated in Piedmont, in northwestern Italy. Being Evangelical—that is to say, first Waldensian, then Huguenot—his family went four times into exile rather than betray their conscience. Leaving France under the compulsion of the revocation (1685) of Protestant liberties granted by the Edict of Nantes, the family settled in the Swiss Canton of Vaud.

Vinet's father (Marc Vinet) was a simple state employee. Moved by a profound sentiment of the commands of God and paternal responsibility, he personally tutored Alexander until his entrance into the Academy of Lausanne. Later, Alexander studied theology in the upper division of this university. In 1817, Vinet accepted the position of teacher of French at the Gymnasium and Paedagogium in Basel. There he was to spend the best years of his life in a "condition of permanent bankruptcy." In July, 1819, he passed his final examination in theology at Lausanne and there was ordained a minister of the state church. Vinet did not enter the active pastorate, but he preached as a supply in the French Reformed Church in Basel and exercised a spiritual ministry for those people who called upon him or wrote to him. In October, 1819, he married his cousin Sophie De la Rottaz, who was to be a worthy and precious life companion.

While in Basel, Vinet came in touch with the Basel Missionary Society, which was a pietistic center. But, as to missions, Vinet felt that it would be better to Christianize Europe before carrying the gospel to a faraway and insignificant place such as Tahiti. As for Pietism, "To me," said Vinet, "the religion of Christ is a religion of light, and the apostles were not pietists." It is our joy and not our sadness that honors God.

In 1822, Vinet's attention fell upon the Religious Awakening of his time. This movement (1810–1850), which passed over Swiss and French Protestantism, was a reaction against the rationalism and worldliness of the former century. "Reason" and "virtue" had been the highest values. The Revival was now emphasizing man's fall, the sovereign grace of God, and deliverance through the gospel. This awakening aimed to place man directly before God and to free the individual from the yoke of state ecclesiasticism. Desiring to examine this movement in the light of Scriptures, Vinet was led to ask himself what was the true nature of Christianity. During a grave illness in 1823, Vinet's entire point of view was changed and he resolved to dedicate his life to Christ. It is impossible, however, to point to a slogan or a motto as a mark of his conversion. His conversion was a spiritual pilgrimage, a gradual transformation under the twofold influence of constant meditation and sorrowful experience with life: "slowly," as he said, he ascended the highest and purest summits.

As a reaction against rationalism and church worldliness, the Awakening unfortunately began to cast the great Christian truths into too narrow a mold, which allowed little scope for the higher culture of the mind. Vinet was struck with the asperities of this extreme dogmatism with its "strange mixture of humility and pride." But when he saw the adherents of the Revival (nicknamed "Mummers" and "Methodists") bravely enduring odious persecutions, Vinet was moved to write his French prize essay *Memoir in Favor of Freedom of Cults,* Paris, 1826. The principle here advocated was not liberty of thinking (which Vinet considered to be beyond the control of any government) but rather the principle of freedom of worship. This book established Vinet's reputation as a thinker, an able writer, and the greatest advocate of liberty of conscience in his time.

There are two bases on which freedom of religion may be philosophically maintained. The first is the impossibility of establishing religious truths by direct evidence, which takes away from the state all rights to impose and to defend them by force; the second is respect for conscience on the ground of God's exclusive right of control over it. It was on this second ground that Vinet took his main stand. Voltaire had pleaded for liberty of conscience in the name of religious indifference. Vinet does so in the name of Christian faith and love.

In consequence of his articles and pamphlets, the gist of which was that it is better to obey God than man, Vinet was tried in absence in his own State of Vaud, fined, and suspended from the ministry in his canton in 1829. This sentence only increased his efforts and influence. The city of Basel showed its appreciation for Vinet's ability and devotion to liberty by giving him its citizenship. While in Basel, Vinet declined several pastorates and professorships. In 1837, however, he received a call as professor at Lausanne, which he finally accepted.

The historical Academy of Lausanne (whose first professors had been Pierre Viret, Guillaume Farel, Konrad Gesner, and Théodore de Bèze) was distinguished for the welcome it gave both to foreigners and to men who preferred exile to slavery: Mickiewicz, the great poet of partitioned Poland, held the Latin professorship; Melegari, an exile from Italy, filled the chair of political economics with an erudition equal to his popularity. There Charles Secrétan was about to commence the course in philosophy in which he endeavored to show the harmony between the gospel and free speculation of thought. The theological faculty (department) commanded at that time the services of Samuel Chappuis, and of J. J. Herzog, who afterward published the *Realenzyklopädie*. There, in 1837, Sainte-Beuve came to offer a course on Port Royal, which anticipated his great work.

Sainte-Beuve professed to have received from the proximity to Vinet and from his sojourn in the land of Vaud an incomparable spiritual profit and a better understanding of "inward Christianity" and of "what it means to be at the school of Christ." But the hopes of Vinet for a conversion of Sainte-Beuve were vain as the great French scholar left. "Since then in reality," writes Seillère, "Sainte-Beuve did hardly seek the truth, if so it be that he ever sought it seriously." Eight years later the great critic, who in the meanwhile had fallen in love with Mme d'Abouville and had been rejected by her, wrote to Vinet: "I have passed into the state of pure critical understanding, and I witness, with a tearful eye, the death of my own heart. I see my condition clearly and I remain calm, cold, and indifferent. I am the typical dead man and I look upon my dead self without its affecting or troubling me in any way. . . . Intellect shines on this cemetery like a dead moon."

In connection with the hoped-for conversion of Sainte-Beuve, we must say that, when speaking of "conversion," Vinet did not mean what the Revival of his day (which emphasized man's fall and salvation by supernatural means) meant by the word "conversion." The Revival, or Awakening, had fixed a certain pattern for the Christian life or way: things ought to happen in a distinct manner and follow a definite course of successive experiences, and not otherwise. Vinet felt that this whole scheme was artificial and factitious: life would lose all naïveté and spontaneity; religion would become mechanical. For him, the religious life is an extremely complex process that does not mechanically follow a rigidly prescribed pattern. We shall see that, for Vinet, faith generally is not a faculty detached from other faculties of man, but a complex spiritual activity in which the whole man is engaged. Repentance, conversion, justification, regeneration, sanctification, cannot be rigidly separated and pointed out singly, nor are they different steps in a chronological succession. They are simply various aspects of one continuous whole, of one perpetual movement of turning to God and to things above. And Vinet could not imagine a love for God that did not spring from gratitude to God. For Vinet, conversion is the work of a lifetime and involves the whole man.

At the Academy of Lausanne, Vinet occupied the chair of practical theology, and taught, among other subjects, the theory of the art of preaching, or homiletics. Yet he did not limit his teaching to theory. He linguistically, or philologically, studied and discussed texts of the Bible with his students. The property of the Bible, for Vinet, is to be not a magic book, not a kind of classroom book, but a book of inspiration, the Book of all divine inspirations. In the light of the external word (the printed Bible) we see, we read the word from within us; and this word encompasses the whole of man and the whole of life. And preaching ought to offer the essence of a Bible passage, explicate it, and apply it to life.

The coming of Vinet to the Lausanne Academy was coincident with a new stress in the unfolding of his religious faith: more and more, in his eyes, our religion, Christianity, is not a science or knowledge, not a system, not an institution, but a *virtus*—a principle of impulsion and life.

On his arrival at Lausanne, Vinet was soon involved in a struggle with state interference in church affairs. At that time the liberal regime, which had come to power through the revolution of 1830, elaborated a revision of the church constitution. A new bill in 1840 strengthened the bonds between state and church. It gave no part to laymen in the church councils; it suppressed the Articles of Faith (that is, the Second Helvetic Confession) and reserved for the government the care of seeing to it that pastors did not abuse their right to doctrinal freedom. It was under these circumstances that Vinet, being unable to accept the abject status of the church before the state, published in French his famous *Essay on the Manifestation of Religious Convictions and Upon the Separation of Church and State*, Paris, 1842.

Vinet opens this work by noting that the most evident illness of modern times is the almost universal absence of convictions not only upon the subject of religion but also in matters of ethics and even politics. The very principle of conviction is wanting. The very fountain of belief seems dried up. Skepticism has become the temperament of the century. Conscience renders no more oracles. Man's paralyzed conscience is silent. The present generation, by dint of understanding everything, has become incapable of passing judgment on anything vital. Everything is probable; everything is plausible. On every basic question the *yes* as well as the *no* is avoided. Nothing is decisive, and because nothing is rejected, nothing is accepted either. Life has no center of gravity, no starting point of action except interest (self-interest, says Vinet) or what is so understood or misunderstood. Self-interest is the only certainty, the only truth that Vinet finds standing in the universal ruins of convictions. The cement of common beliefs no longer binding together the members of the community, men are mingled without being united. Spiritual unity, which is the only true unity, has disappeared; and, each man henceforth gravitating toward himself alone, individualism is the last word of our cultural and social evolution. Man finds himself discouraged and dissatisfied. The void that the absence of religious convictions has caused in the world appears frightful to Vinet. It is undoubtedly true that faith produces spiritual life, he says, but it is equally true that the present absence of faith arises from a decline of inner life. When both faith and life are wanting, how is the one to be awakened by the other? It is in view of this vicious circle that cannot be broken that Vinet decides to agitate the question of professing and the duty of manifesting religious convictions.

Vinet finds men of the present age who desire faith, but he notes that they seek religion not so much because of a serious spiritual want and inner need as because of a vague fear resulting from feeling a sort of impending public danger. To be effectual and fruitful, religious desires must spring from an awareness of moral want. How is this to be awakened? Inner moral life needs religious faith, but religious faith is dependent for its beginning on inward moral life.

With regard to spirituality, most moralists had said, "Do

these things and you shall live!" The gospel, according to Vinet, says, *"You live, therefore you will do these things!"* In other words, in current thought and ordinary ethics, obedience to rules is supposed to open heaven; in the message of Vinet, it is the open heaven (the incarnation) that will impart life.

Vinet already held that the world believes in the opinion of the majority, in tradition, and little in truth. Nowadays there are so many doctrines and so few convictions. Yet Christianity had once been a revolution in this world because it had hoped to establish a race of men who would believe in truth rather than in human opinion or in tradition or in force, and whom the world would regard as solitary fools. But now Vinet's *Essay* went on to affirm that the manifestation, that is, the expression of religious convictions is imperative for every single believer. Proselytism is a duty founded on two mighty motives: gratitude to God for what he has done for us, and charity to our neighbor to whom we owe a share of the truth which we have received. Religion is a sentiment involving affection for, and conviction and research of, absolute truth. True religion is not an individual truth, but a human truth—a truth for all men.

For Vinet, the state as state has no conscience, hence no religion; consequently, an alliance between church and state is pure heresy. If indeed religion is the choice that we make between the world and God, between the visible and the invisible, we must be in a position to choose; but when there is no freedom, there can be no choice, hence no love, no obedience, no Christianity, no religion.

It was also under these circumstances that Vinet, being unwilling to accept the slavish position of the church before the civic law, withdrew from the Vaud Association of Clergy, although not from the national church, because in principle he was opposed to men's separating themselves from existent churches, and in practice he loved his church for what it might become in the future.

In 1845, a new revolution gave the power to the radical party. At its head was a certain Henry Druey (1799–1855), a

scholar and a very able man who had thoroughly assimilated
Hegel's theory on the absolute sovereignty of the state. Henry
Druey's governmental absolutism was combined with a mystic
confidence in "the instinct of the people," namely, of anonymous masses. But Vinet could not understand the divine right
of the many any more than the divine right of one individual.
He felt that "a thing wished for by the greatest number does not
by that fact become either just or social. It may be, on the
contrary, hateful and subversive of all social order." As the new
government tried to rule also the church, Vinet resigned his
position of theological professor, and began to teach French
literature at the Academy, while more than one hundred and
fifty-two ministers (of the two hundred and twenty-five ministers of the state church) seceded from the established church
and founded the Free Evangelical Church of the Canton of
Vaud. Vinet attended its meetings, which were often clandes-
tine, taught at the new Free School of Theology, and took an
active part in the work of the constituent synod. The founding
of the Free Church of the Canton of Vaud is an outstanding
date in the religious history of Europe. On the Old Continent
it was the first time that a modern church was founded on the
principle that it should remain independent and foreign to any
political society, and that its members should be recruited not
according to their birth or citizenship, but in virtue of their free
loyalty. This was achieved in the name of the spiritual nature
of the Christian faith.

On December 3, 1846, Vinet was charged by the state with
having assisted at assemblies held outside the established church
and was discharged from his position at the Academy. As his
health had grown worse, Vinet welcomed the leisure; and, full
of plans concerning projected and unfinished works, he would
fain have retired into the country, but his students besought
him to continue his lectures at the new Independent Seminary,
so he labored on.

On January 28, 1847, Vinet gave his last lecture in theology.
On April 19, he was carried to Clarens, near Montreux, and

there he died on May 4, not even fifty years old. On the eve of his death this great religious figure said to his friends, "Ask for me all graces, even the most elementary; pray for me as for the most unworthy of creatures; ask God that I may live in order to be converted." Later he repeated several times, "Oh, my God, have mercy upon me!" These were his last words. His good wife embraced him and said to him: "Henceforth there will be between us only the name of Jesus. I commit you into his arms." Vinet made a sign of assent and expired.

Vinet never wrote any systematic presentation of his thought. He left his thoughts scattered in essays, book reviews, sermons, discourses, articles, and letters. His ideas are like certain humble yet beautiful Alpine flowers: one must spend much time and energy in searching rocky and often unattractive places—a thing that only a few are disposed to do. Vinet recognized this, for he wrote, "I am not one of those writers who are born translated. I need to be interpreted."

Sainte-Beuve called the style of Vinet "excellent, classical in its way, and with the fragrance of the best literary flowers." Eugène Rambert attributed to Vinet "a unique mode of expression which denotes both a writer formed by the study of great models and a thinker who by himself raises a complete style worthy of any comparison." Philippe Godet sees in Vinet "a writer remarkable for the supreme distinction, atticism, and splendor of style."

II

The Education and Sources
of Thought of Vinet

As WE NOW COME to consider the factors in the education
and forming of Vinet, let us recall that Vinet had his first
schooling under his father. Even as a boy, Vinet had a pronounced interest in reading and literature. At twelve he already
had read all the books belonging to his father; and that meant
all the great French classics. Fortunately Vinet had a cultured
neighbor who owned a bookstore where the young Alexander
could read whatever he found of interest. At the age of thirteen
Vinet was admitted to the second-year class of the lower Academy of Lausanne. He studied letters and philosophy, and soon
he registered in theology.

In later years Vinet thought his studies to have been mediocre. With regard to this, allowance should be made. First,
Vinet was too modest. His later achievements show that he must
have had a good foundation. Secondly, we must recognize the
fact that at that time schools were different from ours today.
The high schools of today are large institutions independent of
colleges and universities. Our high schools are professional
rather than classical. They give our youth the skill to make a
living and all the essentials for being a social success. At the
time of Vinet, high schools and colleges were not entities by
themselves. The high school would prepare pupils for college,
and the college would prepare them generally for the university. A further difference is that today our schools have to please
students, parents, and everybody else in the surrounding com-

munity. Subjects are now watered down and made easy for the students, while in Vinet's time teachers were in authority. Their pupils had to listen to them and to study hard. Finally, there was a greater emphasis on the classics. A knowledge of Greek, Latin, history, and a trip to Italy were the backbone of a man's education. Culture was then understood not as the natural ways of a group or of entire masses but as a certain refinement of a man's mind and taste.

These academic and cultural factors are reflected in Vinet's writings. To make his point, Vinet often uses illustrations taken from ancient Greek and Roman authors, and even uses the word "symbol" with reference to Christian tenets. The reason is that the background of religious thought and scholarship was still classical—even semipagan. For example, a contemporary of Vinet was Friedrich Creuzer. From 1810 to 1812 Creuzer had published a then famous work, *Symbolics and Mythology*, which exhibited the religions of antiquity principally in their symbolical and mythological forms. Therein the ancient gods were not dead but descended upon earth in order to instruct us poor mortals. Apollo himself introduced his own worship at Delphi, and beautiful Ceres invented the use of sacred signs. Symbols were not mere emblems invented by men. They were definite signs of a bond between the divine and the human; and these symbols were given by the gods. Symbols suggested ineffable and spiritual relations. Concerned with myths, Creuzer thought that mythology was the figured expression of a profound theology on the part of ancient peoples. Vinet presupposed a whole classical world which he unconsciously Christianized.

Vinet is generally considered to be a Swiss. Yet, irritated by the injustices which the Swiss United States or Confederation had inflicted upon the city of Basel, Vinet was at times tempted to claim French citizenship. "There is a wide difference between Swiss and French sovereignty," he writes in 1833, "but because of mind and intellectual joys, I would not know which citizenship to prefer."

As for the sources of Vinet's sentiments and thoughts, he

owes much in a general way to the Protestant Reformers. He had some of Luther's sense of urgency and, while writing his *Memoir,* Vinet did not cease from repeating Luther's phrase, "I cannot help it." Vinet also had the ancient Reformed sense of risk and referred to Calvin's constant walking on the edge of frightful precipices, that is, between contrasting thoughts and contrary policies. We shall see in Chapter VII how Vinet the Christian critic will transcend Romanticism, yet he owes much to its founders: Rousseau, Chateaubriand, and especially Mme de Staël. Of these something must here be said as well as of Thomas Erskine, De Wette, Philip A. Stapfer, and Blaise Pascal, who influenced the formulations of Vinet's thoughts.

I

MME DE STAEL

Germaine Necker, baroness of Staël-Holstein, was the first distinguished Protestant writer of modern France. The only daughter of the unsuccessful minister of King Louis XVI, she was born in 1766 at Paris and died there in 1817. She was a disciple of J. J. Rousseau (1712–1778), for whom the primitive and primordial force of man is sentiment. Rousseau had exhorted men to let themselves be inspired by the grand spectacles of nature and guided by the inner voice of conscience, which is a divine instinct. When the French Revolution came, Mme de Staël accepted it as being the vindication of her beloved father's views. She was disliked and even persecuted by Napoleon on account of her political liberalism and friendship with Benjamin Constant. With a similar background, that is, Protestant parentage and education, Constant (1767–1830) was a vigorous thinker, the typical liberal for whom individuality is of such value that it accepts no compromise. With J. J. Rousseau and Chateaubriand, Mme de Staël supplied numerous ideas to Vinet.

Our reader will recall that Chateaubriand (1768–1848) sought to prove that Christianity is the most human and poetic of all religions, and the most favorable to liberty. Christianity had inspired literature, arts, agriculture, and even the most abstract sciences. For him, the Christian religion is a sort of passion, altogether irrational. Nothing is more divine than Christian ethics. Chateaubriand was essentially an artist. But, whereas he aimed at humanizing Christianity, Mme de Staël spoke of Christianizing humanity. She felt that the small number of ideas considered necessary and evident in the previous rationalistic century would never satisfy the spirit and heart of man. Metaphysical precision not only does not meet men's moral affections but is altogether incompatible with human nature. She could not share the religion of those dry minds which were seeking to prove Christianity scientifically. According to Mme de Staël, words cannot express the heartfelt mystery of existence. Reasonings simply mark the end of reasoning; and where reasoning ends, true certainty begins. Just as there had been truths of faith, and then truths of reason, now for her there are truths of sentiment. These are so strong and intense that they involve our whole being. The Infinite acts upon us, lifts and frees us from temporality. Religion is nothing unless it is everything, that is, unless it fills our whole existence. Christianity is nothing unless we have such a faith in the Invisible, such a devotion and loftiness of desire, as will enable us to triumph over the vulgar tendencies of our nature.

Mme de Staël defined Protestantism as being the union of a living faith with a critic's discriminating mind. Reason cannot wrong such a faith, nor such a faith wrong reason. Christianity had been first founded, then altered, then examined by the Reformers and understood anew by Protestants. Hence we must ever reexamine Christianity not with a view of destroying it but in order to found ourselves upon inner convictions and not on beliefs borrowed from others. A preestablished harmony between truth and reason brings truth and reason together.

As our reader has noticed, Mme de Staël sometimes is opposed to reason and sometimes she is favorable to it. But let us not seek or expect from her rational consistency. Like Vinet's, her writings abound in antitheses, contrasts, and self-contradictions. Her books are to be felt and lived rather than reasoned about. Like Vinet, she intended to minister not to reason but to life; and life, after all, is a mass of contradictions. Men with unselfish affections and truly religious thoughts, says Mme de Staël, are the true priests, and nothing will divide such men. An abyss separates men who are led by calculations from men who are guided by sentiment. Here, and not in matter of opinions, is found the radical difference between men. It is possible that someday a miracle may occur and Christians be theologically, politically, and morally united, but before this wonder happens, men who have a heart and obey it must in the meantime mutually respect one another.

II

THOMAS ERSKINE

While Vinet was in Basel, he came upon and read the *Remarks on the Internal Evidence for the Truth of Revealed Religion* of Thomas Erskine (1788–1870), a Scottish lawyer. This book so impressed Vinet that he said, "If by principle I did not hate the expression, 'I am of Apollos or of Cephas,' I should readily say, 'I am of Erskine.'" Erskine, in his turn, "learned much from Vinet" in his later years.

This work of Erskine's is one of the great interpretations of the mystic and moral side of Calvinism and of the psychological conditions that correspond with the doctrine of the grace of God, that is, of his loving-kindness in operation for us.

The aim of Erskine's *Remarks* was to illustrate the harmony that subsists between Christianity and the moral facts that lie around us and within us. In his view, the proper criterion of the truth of Christianity is not historical criticism or any external authority, but rather the "sense of moral obligation." It was for this purpose of elucidating and enforcing our moral obligations and aspirations that God disclosed himself in the fact of Christ, whose sacrifice is a standard by which we may estimate both the divine goodness and our own guilt. When the conscience thus comes to be fully enlightened, nothing short of this exhibition can produce peace of mind.

As it is a law of our inner constitution that the foundation of our faith becomes necessarily the mold of our characters, he who truly rests his hope on Christ's atonement and its spiritual excellence becomes, through conformity to Jesus, a partaker of the character of God. The great argument for Christianity lies in the sanctifying influence of its doctrines. The great argument against it lies in the unsanctified lives of its professors. Hence the habit of viewing the Christian doctrine and the Christian character as two separate things is a pernicious tendency. The opposition to "spiritual Christianity" has its true and principal roots not in reason but in the moral will of the unbeliever: the uncompromising holiness of the Evangelical principles generally provokes a reaction on the part of human nature.

III

DE WETTE

Born in a simple village manse of Thuringia, Wilhelm De Wette (1780–1849) was the most distinguished representative of Biblical scholarship of that period. Because of the purity of his character, the sincerity of his convictions, and the conscientiousness of his work, De Wette was called "the Nathanael of Modern Theology." He first published several volumes on the Old Testament (1806–1817), everywhere forcefully opposing the naturalistic explanations of miracles, which the rationalists had put in vogue. He eloquently defended the moral grandeur and poetic inspiration of the Scriptures.

According to De Wette, the religious sentiment is the means by which man rises from the finite to the Infinite. Religious sentiment participates in the nature of aesthetic feeling and is independent of reason. Religious sentiment itself is neither true nor false. It does not procure for man any knowledge of the truth. It reveals nothing to us, but by the flight or *élan* that it communicates, it calms and transports us by turns. Dogma is the visible form that the religious feeling puts on. Religious sentiment incarnates itself in symbols, legends, and myths. In order to understand these dogmatic or theological monuments of the past, we should free them of their symbolic wrappings and show the religious and aesthetic sentiments that gave them birth.

These theories naturally met the opposition of shortsighted theologians, and in 1819, De Wette lost the professorship he had held in Berlin University since 1810. He retired to Weimar, where he collected in five tomes the voluminous *Correspondence of Luther,* which was published in 1825–1828. He also devoted himself to *Ethics* (three volumes, 1819–1823), concluding that only a life rooted in God can make a man understand and solve the problem of human destiny. In 1822, De Wette was called to the University of Basel to expound the New Testament, on which he was later to publish a *Concise Commentary* in three large volumes (1836–1848). This undertaking changed considerably De Wette's concept of faith. He came to say that, rather than an exaltation of sentiment, faith is a spiritual force that results from Christ's work to animate Christian men and women.

As soon as De Wette arrived at the University of Basel, where Vinet had been offering courses in French Literature since 1819, Vinet went to hear him for six months and even translated one of De Wette's discourses into French. It is impossible to say to what extent De Wette influenced the thought of Vinet, but a sure thing is that he revealed to Vinet that exegesis, that is, the study and exposition of Scripture, ought to be the mother and not the servant of our religious thought. "The lessons of De Wette," Vinet writes, "caused me great joy. I felt that for the first time I was doing exegesis (that is, finding out what a Bible passage originally meant). We read Paul's letters to the Galatians and Romans in Greek. De Wette has profound and fine views and the gift of making us see the connection of passages and grasp the whole. His exposition is precise and methodical. De Wette's literary and theological honesty is as remarkable as his talent and erudition."

As De Wette's opinion was that reason uses the language of philosophy while the heart uses the language of symbols, the gap or antinomy between exact knowledge and religious sentiment was for him an unsolvable problem. De Wette thought that a life of Jesus could never be written because God's providence had willed that such a history should remain shrouded in a perpetual chiaroscuro. A little less historical certainty, rather than shake our faith, ought to incite us the more to penetrate from the visible into the invisible world above, where we are to find our true objects of faith and the sources of that life which never tarnishes.

For Vinet also, faith will be less an elation of feeling than a spiritual force that fills and animates us. Faith is the result of the incarnation, of the work of Christ on earth—the reconciliation of man to God. Vinet believes in the intimate union of God and humanity in Christ the Mediator—the new Adam of a new kind of men and immortal King of the future. Vinet finds the supreme and only solution of philosophical problems in the incarnation, that is, in God's Word or Reason (logos) becoming man in Jesus Christ. Philosophy seeks impersonal reason. The Christian believes in that personal and supreme Reason which is Jesus Christ. Thus Vinet transcends, that is, goes beyond, De Wette's dualism between reason, which destroys the ancient dogma, and the aesthetic needs of the Romanticists, who rebuilt it for sentimental reasons. Vinet will undoubtedly ease, if not solve, the conflict between new exact knowledge (science) and ancient religious symbolism.

IV

Philip Albert Stapfer

Philip Albert Stapfer (1766–1840) had been professor at the Institute of Bern, then Minister of Public Education, and finally Plenipotentiary Ambassador of the Swiss Republic to

Paris (1800–1803), where he settled for the rest of his life.

Stapfer had been greatly impressed by the philosophy of Kant, whom he was one of the first to introduce into France. Stapfer, however, thus completed the celebrated formula: "Two things, Kant has said, fill my soul with an ever and ever increasing admiration and respect: the starry sky *above me* and the moral law *within me.* Kant could have added: and the fulfillment of the moral law in the person of Jesus *outside of me.*" In fact, Stapfer had learned from Kant the limits of pure reason, and accepted, by practical reason and moral sense, the Christian solution of the religious question and life problem. The words of the Johannine Christ: "If it be one's will to do the will of God, he shall know whether my teaching proceeds from God or whether I speak from myself" (John 7:17), had always appeared to Stapfer as the real criterion of the truth of Christianity.

Stapfer's idea of faith is important. Already in 1797 he had written, "Religious faith is a moral condition, a complex state, resulting from the active and harmonious cooperation of all the forces of the soul." Vinet remarked, "This assertion is even more important since, in the eyes of Stapfer, this cooperation is not less the token of certainty in religious matters than the condition under which religious faith is something better than a certainty."

Stapfer, who possessed a prodigious erudition, heartily sympathized with the Evangelical Awakening of his time, and presented its scholarly and philosophical aspect. But this Christian Socrates left only scattered articles, which were later collected in two French volumes of *Miscellanies,* 1844.

V

Blaise Pascal

Already in 1832, Vinet had offered in Basel a course on Pascal. In 1844 and 1845, taking advantage of the new edition of Pascal's *Thoughts* by Prosper Faugère, he gave new lectures on the great Jansenist at Lausanne Academy. Vinet also wrote articles on Pascal for the Paris weekly *The Sower* (*Le Semeur*) and for the *Swiss Review*. When Victor Cousin came to charge Pascal with skepticism (Pyrrhonism), it was Vinet, "one of those faithful friends according to Paul," who took the cause of this great Christian thinker most directly in hand and showed forth the greatness of Pascal's religion.

As our reader recalls, Pascal (1623–1662) had planned a great apologetic of Christianity. Of this projected work unfortunately Pascal left but fragments, known as *Pensées*. In these remains he proposed to follow a course all his own:

The given fact is human nature: man is a monstrous assemblage of contrasting elements, of greatness and misery, of nobility and abasement. Yet if man opens his soul to grace, he finds the living God of Abraham and Jacob. In other words, when man, not by reasoning, but by an act of will, yields his moral obedience to the will of God, the Christian faith and life come to abide in him. The believer realizes then that the source of his misery was a reversal of the inner powers composing man and that his life becomes orderly and harmonious when it is reorganized by divine grace. The Christian conversion is a reality. Through it we enter the supernatural order of charity (above matter and mind) where God again masters our heart, which, in its turn, masters our senses and reason. Christianity is not a piece of the supernatural mechanically laid upon human nature. It is the supernatural interpenetrating and re-forming man. The Christian religion alone is therefore the explanation and the remedy for the problems and evils of man's existence.

The study of Pascal occupied Vinet all his life. As Pascal's *Abridgment of the Life of Jesus* had been discovered in Utrecht by M. Van der Hoeven, and published in Paris by Faugère, a friend lent the booklet to Vinet, who on his deathbed still found the energy to review it for the Paris weekly *Le Semeur*. Shortly after, Sainte-Beuve wrote in *Le Journal des débats*, "If one would gather together the articles of M. Vinet on Pascal, one could have, in my opinion, the most exact conclusions that can possibly be attained about this great character who is so much disputed." In effect, some friends had Vinet's articles and fragments of courses appear in French in book form under the title *Studies on B. Pascal,* Paris, 1848.

The nature of his mind, temperament, and life made it possible for Vinet to understand the noble and prodigious Jansenist genius: the penetrating analysis of human nature, the attachment of the heart to the need of both faith and evidence, a natural vein of melancholia, a passion in reason and reason in passion, an unflinching sincerity, a guarded yet powerful imagination, graduated in the stern school of illness and accomplishing vast intellectual labors while contending with an incurable bodily malady—all these traits are common to the author of the *Pensées* and to Vinet.

However, besides mere affinity of temperament, Pascal and Vinet had a basic element in common: a deep, personal, and authentic religious experience. In both cases the subject of faith and sentiment was the person of Jesus Christ. Hence, their faith, in spite of different environments and denominations, led Pascal and Vinet to the same results. It made of them both not only admirable believers but the initiators and the protagonists of a common achievement in spiritual history. The analysis and exercise of their Christian sentiment unfolded for them a new psychology. They attributed to religious life and knowledge a medium or organ of its own and a distinct origin. This origin is sentiment or intuition; this medium is "the heart" for Pascal, "the conscience" for Vinet. This is the fruitful novelty which among French-speaking Protestants has ever since bound together the names of Pascal and Vinet.

III

The Vindication of Christianity

I

THE NEW ORIENTATION

THE GLORY of Alexander Vinet is to have been the creator and the inspirer of a new orientation that freed French-speaking Protestants from the burden of a dead ecclesiasticism and from the crudity of the revivalism of that time. Vinet interpreted this twofold liberation through his spiritual depth, his religious amplitude, his keen comprehension of the universality of religion, and his sensitive receptivity to what is characteristic and unique in Christianity.

According to Vinet, Luther and Calvin did not once and for all renovate the church. They simply stated principles and affirmed the condition of all future reforms. In his view, the Protestant Reformation ought to be permanent in the church. For the Reformation is simply the basic ideas and forces of Christianity constantly redemanding their place; it is Christianity restoring itself by its own energies so that at all times the Re-formation of Christianity ought to be still in progress.

Although Vinet had thus the conviction that new forms ought to be sought for Christian ethics and new expressions ought to be found for Christianity, his premature death did not permit the achievement of this mission. However, he became as a leaven for the successive developments, not under the form of a unified and well-defined doctrinal system, but by the creative and informing spirit of his rich personality.

For Vinet, formulas are not the basis and the sure fabric of religion. Only when applied to and resting on life can theology give living expression to religion. Vinet has pronounced these bitter words: a church may die of spiritual starvation although being fully orthodox, while "neology," that is, doctrinal novelty, endangers the existence of a church much less than does dogmatic exactness. On the other hand, Vinet emphasized the fact that when the epoch of a spiritual awakening comes, its new religious fervor develops itself on "the rough and rugged soil of orthodoxy and under the shadow of those mysteries which confound human reason." The middle and easy way is indeed unbearable and powerless in religion: "Christianity, in this commonplace, bourgeois century, tends to become commonplace, ordinary, bourgeois. The tragic element, which is essential to Christianity, little by little disappears."

The common pretension to understand everything in the Christian religion is absurd: to understand everything is to understand God; and to understand God would be God himself. A religion made in the image of man is false. Hence, Vinet always opposes both orthodox and heterodox intellectualisms, for he sees in them the danger of a domination of purely human thoughts. Sound doctrinal theology should be to religious life what science is to nature. Theology should not impose itself on religion more than science imposes itself on nature. If theology seeks to penetrate the mystery of religion, its first duty is to respect it; the gaze of the heart turned toward Jesus Christ— this is always the essential fact, the living truth.

II

THE PERSON AND WORK OF CHRIST

No one more than Vinet perceived the unreasonableness of the gospel. He held that to lower Christianity to the level of common sense is to deprive the truth of its mysterious power.

Hence, following the earliest preachers of the Awakening, Vinet emphasizes that which remained hidden under the veil of the old orthodox dogma.

Christianity is mysterious because it is true. As with the mountains—the higher they are, the deeper shadow they cast— the gospel is obscure and mysterious in proportion to its sublimity and truth. Thus Vinet stresses the paradoxical and the mysterious in Christianity, and yet its necessity, efficacy, and truth. We find in him Pascal's bitter severity: the gospel attracts by that which revolts; it is powerful by its very foolishness. For the Christian the superfluous is the necessary. And the mediocre is the false, because the religion of a lofty God cannot tolerate mediocrity (Isa. 55:8–9). By this prophetic stress on paradox and metaphor, Vinet will show vital truths, for he will emphasize the personal and unique character of Christianity as against the conventional and rationalistic character of current religion.

Vinet markedly insists that Golgotha is the center and the whole of the gospel. Vinet loves to unfold the folly of the cross: there God is in Christ calling the world unto himself; there in Christ, and for the first time, God fully reveals to us the immensity of his love; there a God who is love explains a God who dies; and a God who dies for us is the one God in whom mankind is able to believe. God could not reach us without putting on our nature, becoming one of us, and summing up all our misery in himself. Yes, love is a mystery, the greatest of all mysteries, and the key to all mysteries, having itself no key. In the least impulse of a true love there is more than can be fathomed by the most penetrating intellect. Love, like life, eludes all explanations. Love is its own reason; it is from the beginning with God; it is God; nothing has preceded it, nor begotten it. To ask it to give account of itself is vain, impossible; as well might it be said to God, "Who made Thee?"

On the cross, God was both just and merciful, striking himself for sinful man, giving himself to us. We may defy the human mind to devise any other plan of deliverance, reconciliation, and restoration that is worthy of God, yes, worthy of man, and consequently not inefficacious and illusory. We may connect this mystery with a more general mystery—the mystery of solidarity. Mankind is one solid, one unity. In it sin is transmissible, reversible. Why should not righteousness and love be so too? Here reasoning has not the first place. Love can be understood only by love. And from the heart, reason must receive light: first love, someday you shall understand!

The sum of divine revelation is that God is love, and love cannot help loving. Yes, the gospel attracts by what seems at first repulsive. It is powerful by its very folly. Thus, on the cross we see the ethics of God in all its absoluteness and inviolability, a revelation to man that tells of the justice, holiness, and goodness of God. Only by this Means is revelation an active and powerful force that will awaken us to a new life.

The coming of Christ is not a mere development of history, but rests in the purpose and initiative of God himself. Christ is God's objective manifestation and the token of God's lovingkindness. "God reveals himself," says Vinet, "not so much by telling us as by showing us what he is." God delivers us by showing himself. The great revelation of Christianity is "God manifested in the flesh." God wished to attract man unto himself in this way. As for the incarnation itself, that is, as for the manner of the union of the divine element and the human element in Christ—this is a mystery about which Vinet does not even try to speculate. Vinet's eyes are fixed on the cross: the drama on Golgotha is essentially religious and moral, and can be seized only by a man who is under the burden of sin. Metaphysical and rational explanations about the origin, the nature, and the work of the person of Christ are useless to Christian consciousness. What matters is the fact. The gospel presents a fact, a Person, a new creation. The fact is the starting point, the basis, and the substance of all its message. The eternal Christ does not say, "I show the way, I teach the truth, I will tell you where life is," but he says, "I am the way, the truth, and the life" (John 14:6). Let us therefore not put

Christendom in the place of Christ. To be a Christian is to belong to Christ and to live in fellowship with him.

But, although stressing the fact that it is the conscience that recognizes the Evangelical tenets of man's condemnation and of Christ's salvation as facts of inner experience, Vinet never gave up the objective element in Christianity for the sake of subjectivity and mere psychology. On the contrary, Vinet felt the peril of the coming naturalism. There is a kind of physiology of Christianity to which some reduce the whole of apologetic reasoning; the former explains humanly a work that Christianity explains divinely. Nothing so much weakens the authority of Christianity, nothing injures its cause so much in the midst of men, as to make it a link in a chain of historical developments and evolutions which, in truth, Christianity has broken. That circumstances—that is to say, Providence—hollowed out, beforehand, a channel for this divine stream is what the most scrupulous of believers will easily grant; but it is essential not to mistake the source from whence the stream flowed. No natural development and historical evolution, Jewish or Greek, could explain the existence of Christianity. Whatever the progress of ancient thought, there was always an infinite distance between it and Christian thought; and only the Infinite itself could fill the infinite. It is all over with Christianity in the world when men agree to believe the contrary, and to force a supernatural fact into one of the divisions of philosophy of history. As far as Vinet is concerned, he much prefers for the Christian religion an outrageous negation to an admiration confined within such limits. Christianity is nothing if it be not like Melchizedek—without father and mother here below, without earthly ancestry.

The Christian religion is God placing himself in relation with man, the Creator with the creature, the Infinite with the finite. The religion that leads to God can be but from God. To proclaim, however objectively, the justice of God as satisfied by God himself on the cross and hence conclude the certainty of subjective deliverance does not suffice. The human conscience hesitates to concede that a faith without moral results can be the only condition of salvation. Such a faith remains in the condition of belief, something outward that does not act on man's inner being. In order to be effective, God's rescue must become (from the external grace that frees the sinner from self-condemnation) an inner grace that frees man from evil. The negative and objective deliverance must be followed by a positive and subjective deliverance. Through our contemplation of Christ, the work of God in Christ becomes, above all, a work of inner renewal. We are really freed only when we have made of Christ our sanctification, and die to the power of sin as Christ himself died because of sin.

Here again Vinet unfolds the Christian fact of salvation (which is a reduction of man's sinful self) in paradox and metaphor rather than in terms of common human understanding. But the logic of Vinet's religion is also the logic of conscience: if there were no obscurities in Christianity, the heart would entrust rational intelligence with everything. Abstract terms cannot encompass and reflect all the fullness and depth of life. A religion that should seem reasonable to everyone could not be the true religion. Its general assent granted without resistance would not even be a demonstration in its favor.

This accounts for the value that Vinet gives to philosophy. Knowledge is limited by the terms of comparison and can therefore grasp neither the unconditional nor the absolute. Speculative ideas cannot reach the truth because the primary truth is of an ethical nature. It is the subconscious that determines our line of reasoning: "Pride is stronger than reason." Hence the decisive proofs of objective truth are more easily found in the depths of the human being than in the domain of the mind. The philosophy of a man is but the intellectual product of that man's moral nature. Religious conviction and doubt are not merely two attitudes of the mind but two states of the inner life, and so long as the soul is not restored, there will be many truths that we shall not believe firmly. Purely formal logic is merely instrumental and can disprove anything according to one's will. Vinet was struck by Pascal's "tremendous" expression, "The will, organ of belief": what in the sphere of human opinion is called faith is but will applied to the object of speculation, whereas the exact measure of the intensity of this faith is but the force of the will.

III

Vindication of the Christian Religion

When Vinet appeared, the Protestant apologetics, the art of vindicating Christianity, was in a most miserable state. It combined the most heterogeneous processes and techniques: now it was imposing the Holy Bible and the dogmas by way of authority, now it was taking from history the proofs of the supernatural, now it explained all miracles naturally, now it was trying to prove faith by a syllogistic method. To this heteroclite collection of arms taken from the arsenals of the seventeenth and eighteenth centuries, Vinet opposes Pascal's method: the psychological and moral, the internal apologetics.

Vinet does not address himself arbitrarily to this or that side of human nature in order to make it the support of an abstract theory of Christianity, but he penetrates what is characteristic and vital in man. He understands that, because of the effects it produces in the believer, the Christian life has no better advocate than itself. He gradually develops this idea with a truly marvelous demonstrative power and richness of outlook. To the partisans of authority he opposes the duty of personal convictions; to those of historic proofs he shows the insufficiency of history; to rationalists he reveals the limits of reason and the uncertainty of dialectics; against all, finally, he reclaims the rights and competence, in religious matters, of the "heart," namely, of the will bent by grace and submitted to a conscience enlightened by God. With keen intuition Vinet sums up the whole of the gospel in the person of Jesus Christ and the whole of man in the conscience. Without any intermediary, to place Jesus Christ in face of the conscience and the conscience in face of Jesus Christ, and by the immediacy of this encounter to awaken man to the sense of both his misery and greatness—this is the first task of Vinet.

The medium of truth, the channel from the divine to the human, the possibility of inner renewal and sublime freedom, rest in the conscience. By "conscience" Vinet does not mean the moral law which, being a body of notions and a complex result, changes according to time, country, education, and person. By "conscience" Vinet means an elemental fact, the sentiment of obligation in its greatest purity and most perfect abstraction, namely, *the sense of the necessity to make our actions harmonize with our inner conviction* as to right and wrong. Vinet thinks it is amazing that there should be something (the conscience) planted in man besides the self. And with what right, for what purpose, is the conscience there? This nonself, this inalienable associate of the self which some men would gladly dispense with, this duality in human beings, this unknown something, this agent which claims obedience, has given and still gives untold trouble to conscientious philosophers. Yet conscience (inalienable possession that constitutes the identity of moral man, since deprived of this organ, man would no longer be man) is the one only possible basis of man's restoration.

It is on this foundation that God reconstructs man. For between the conscience and Christ there is a kind of *pre-established harmony*. Conscience is only the permanent and ineffaceable impress of a powerful hand, which, having once inflicted on us this impress, has removed its pressure, or, rather, from under which an inimical force has torn man away. The hand is now absent; the impression remains. Thus man bears in his secret depths an inscription written, as it were, in a secret or invisible ink which only the fire reveals. The gospel is the fire, and by its warmth we are going to read again the divine characters once traced on man's inner being.

Like Pascal, Vinet starts his vindication of our religion by calling our attention to the condition of man: man had once been created for the glory of God—his Creator. This was the end in the pursuit of which man ought to have found his happiness and dignity. But man abandoned this aim, and, wishing to be equal to God, fell into a state of utter misery and is now like a deposed king who remembers his lost kingdom. Vinet is fully aware that "this teaching of man's fall irritates human pride." Yet it is under the compulsion of a deep need for rehabilitation that man worked at creating some religion that would reestablish his broken relation with God. As a matter of fact, the wants of man are great: Man is ignorant of divine things: he needs a religion that enlightens him. He is oppressed by the evils of his life and by the uncertainty of his future destiny: he needs a religion that comforts him. Lastly, he is a sinner: he needs a religion that renews him. "Happiness is not a fruit of our nature, and does not grow spontaneously on the stem of life; it must needs be grafted there by a divine hand."

In order to answer these needs, some have given their faith to a religion satisfying *imagination* through the admiration of nature, and they take delight in extolling it as the image or expression of the Eternal Being. The satisfaction offered by this cult, however, is deceiving, hence transitory. From the high spectacle where imagination has lifted him, man soon falls within himself and feels only the enormous disproportion between the universe, which is full of the Lord's glory, and his own inner being, which is void of Him.

Others seek God by way of *intellect,* or intelligence, but these too fall into deception. This is the experience of all systems and ages. When the consistent philosopher is placed face-to-face with the Infinite, he ends by seeing realities as dissolved—the most universal certainties vanish away, and his very individuality becomes (as with the doubting Descartes) a problem. Absolute skepticism (Pyrrhonism) is but the despair of reason. Thus this religion of man, made wholly and only of thought, has not enlightened, changed, or comforted him.

Experiencing this, many persons reject these idle speculations of the mind and acknowledge no religion but that of *feeling,* that is, of love to God. But they soon find that in fact the love of God (if by this they mean a love real, earnest, dominant, and lasting) is not natural to the heart of man. Love, true love of God, is a love of his truth, of his holiness, of his entire will; true love is that which purifies and renews the conscience.

This brings us finally to the fourth religion that man makes for himself, that of *conscience.* More serious men indeed seek the solution of the great problem of life in a religion of the conscience, in that impulse which urges us to do the will of God, to resemble him, and prescribes us to live for God. But the conscience is not God; it is simply his ambassador. Hence the urging of the conscience (apart from God) can inspire us only to despair. This fact is witnessed by the experience and history of mankind: the sentiment of guilt has such power over the heart of man that he had recourse even to the abominable practice of shedding human blood without having this sacrifice put man at peace with himself.

None of these "natural" religions is able to give man the good he has lost. Their impotence is partly due to the fact that each of these religions of man is founded on but one of the faculties or functions of man. The whole truth is only to be apprehended and grasped by the whole man. Real religion should address itself to the whole of man, to all his capacities, to all his functions, and unite into a living unity the contrasting elements of human nature.

Natural religion teaches us, however, two great truths: that there is a God, and that man is made for God and ought to reascend toward him; but man can renounce neither his sinfulness nor God; his alienation and perversion drag him with the rest of this world.

As man cannot create a religion that enlightens, strengthens, and renews him, such a religion has to be offered to him from without. Man by himself cannot reconcile himself to God; hence God must come to man. As we saw, God comes to us in Christ. This religion is Christianity. The Christian religion offers to man the two great goods that he unconsciously needs: the *forgiveness* of a God in face of whom no human sacrifice was able to acquit the conscience, and a moral *renovation* that frees man from the tyranny of evil. The token of forgiveness is Christ dying on the cross; the mark of man's inner renewal is God's grace, the communication of his Spirit and love.

For Vinet, the Fall of man is not a mere legend and old fable, but rather the symbolic expression of a living reality around us and a fact of conscience within us. This Fall is perpetual. It does not consist in the straying of man's intellect or imagination, but in the straying of his heart and will. The Fall did and does involve the very center of man's personality. By telling of deliverance and dedication of the will to Christ as Lord, Christianity saves man's very center, hence the whole man. This idea leads us to tell briefly of what might be called "Vinet's philosophy."

To his volume of *Essays of Moral Philosophy and Religious Ethics,* Paris, 1837, Vinet places, as one of the two epigraphs, Pascal's words, "One does not show his greatness by being at one extreme, but rather in touching both extremes at once and filling up all in between." Vinet's Introduction to these *Essays* (which are "about the reduction of dualities") is in its turn preceded by the New Testament words found in Eph. 1:10: *anakephalaiosasthai ta panta en to Christo,* which Vinet understood to mean, "Christ is the solution of all contradictions." These two epigraphs represent "Vinet's philosophy."

The world, life, and thought, as we saw, are full of contrasts and conflicts. These dualities remain irreducible. In all times the aim of all philosophies is to reduce to unity these opposites. But philosophy has as yet not found that mysterious *quid*— something capable of binding the contrasting facts and opposite principles. The Christian, says Vinet, cannot ignore and bypass these problems: the idea of keeping in oneself both a philosopher and a Christian who do not understand each other and mutually ignore each other is absurd. As it is impossible to carry within oneself two men, there are but two possible attitudes: either philosophy must be born from religion, or religion must be born from philosophy. The solution is found in Jesus Christ. By responding to him and accepting him, our inner nature is brought to unity.

The peace that he gives puts an end to the troubles of intellect, to the anxieties of the conscience, to the torments of the heart. The source of all conflicts, splits, and dualities was, indeed, the profound opposition between what God demands and what the human heart offers; between what God wills and what man wills; between duty and the well-rooted desire to reach happiness by following our own wills. "The 'crime of Adam,' which each and every man repeats and confirms, consists in saying, 'There is a God, but I will act as though there were none.' All evils," says Vinet, "spring from this one source. All the pride of modern wisdom can be summed up in these words, 'The salvation of mankind comes from mankind.' "

No theory, no human philosophy, but only Christianity reconciles these conflicts, for only the Christian finds, through Christ and faith, happiness in doing what God commands, and hence that inner continuity and integration which man would seek elsewhere in vain. This is not a theory, not an abstraction, but a fact of Christian experience: the gospel without hesitation brings forth contradictory truths and conciliates them by absorbing them into a higher truth. Christ is the solution and transcendence of all contradictions. Man and the Christian truth are created one for the other: the truth of the gospel corresponds and intimately unites itself to the deepest element of our human nature and creates unity therein; thus "our soul does not discover the truth, but recognizes it," and by that very fact finds itself in it. As we will soon see, truth is not a form but a substance, and there is but one way to *know* the truth: it is to *be in* the truth.

IV

A Spiritual Vision of Love and Truth

VINET RECOGNIZES three orders of reality: the material, the intellectual, and the moral. He thought, however, that there is an infinitely greater distance between the moral level and the intellectual level than there is between the intellectual level and the material level. In this Vinet follows Pascal, who had said this: All material bodies—the firmament, the stars, the earth, pressed together—would not yield the least thought and hence are not equal to the least mind; for the mind knows all these things and itself besides, while all material things put together know absolutely nothing. The mind therefore belongs to a higher order. And yet all minds and all intellectual products—pressed together—would not yield the least movement of true love and hence are not equal to the least feeling of Christian charity. Charity belongs to an infinitely more exalted order, the supernatural.

When Vinet speaks of the things that are above, he does not mean the things of another world, but the things of a sphere different from our habitual thoughts. They are not things necessarily above our heads, but above our natural feelings. They are the dispositions of a heart renewed by the Spirit from above. They are all the sentiments, motives, and impulses that constitute a new being. To love the things that are above is to love God himself, who is above; to submit our life to God, to seek him, and to find him in all things.

The sort of love most men speak about, mere humanitarian love, would not raise us above animals. Love deserves the holy name of love, only when, being perfected by the Spirit of God, it has become charity. The love of God, if we understand by it a real, earnest, controlling love, is not natural to the heart of man. The natural thing for man is always to raise an idol in the place of the true God. Nothing less is done. This idol, which man constantly creates, sometimes has a name, sometimes none; but in both cases alike, the idol is our own heart. All adorations, except that of God manifested in the flesh, contain this idolatry. All these adorations prostrate us before an altar of which our ego is the divinity. If God alone be not adored, everything will before long be God to us, except God himself. Only the cross of Christ can overthrow the human ego. We must in a certain sense become mad in order to become wise; that is, reason must needs humble itself in the presence of things that had never entered into the heart of man and which God has prepared for them that love him. Sovereign love in God, pure love in man, such is the only motive worthy of religion, and worthy of man. God is not like a human legislator. He is the spiritual Being who requires the worship of the heart—a worship in spirit and truth, produced and supported by love. It is for this end that Jesus Christ restored to man the divine image and reinstated him by love alone. Love opens the mind to thoughts so high, so new, that they must seem folly to those who do not accept them.

To love God is at once the culmination and the decline of the *me*. To love is at once to give all and to have all; we give our hearts, but the reward of that gift lies in the gift itself; and the sacrifice of the *me,* in the mysterious state of the soul, is itself the delight of the *me*. The love of man for the love of God, the love of the image of God in every man; the love that willingly makes itself small and gracefully steps aside—true Christian love, in short, can spring only from the mystery of the cross. A divine violence has to be done to that human heart which can be conquered and gained only by violence. Man had inverted all his relations with God; God in his turn inverted all his relations with man. Man had made himself God; God made himself man. Man had refused everything to God; God gave himself to man in the person of Jesus Christ. The cross raised on Golgotha has shown to men a prodigy of charity in an earnest of reconciliation.

In the life of every man the distinct offer of salvation creates a crisis that terminates differently according to the different dispositions it meets in men. With a holy violence the grace of God seeks to force man to return to the divine law by the way of the divine loving-kindness; it snatches man from the world to give him to God. In a word, it deals the most formidable blow to human self-respect and pride. The morality of the gospel is not the gradual and partial restoration of man. It does not add virtue to virtue till the frame be full; but it throws into man a new principle of life and action (the love of God) by bringing before man God himself becoming man in Jesus Christ for man's deliverance. Man begins to detach himself from the things of this world only when he has learned to know something better. Love is the principle of the New Covenant. In that new people, which God has made in his own image, love is the new principle of obedience, the supreme law, the spirit of all laws. Everything in this economy of God is marked with the stamp of love. If faith saves, it is because it produces hope and charity in men.

To Vinet, when Christianity speaks of love, it means spiritual love. To love spiritually means to love as God loves and as he desires to be loved. The Christian loves God in every human life, and loves every life in God. He sees all things with God's eyes, and loves, so to speak, with the very heart of God. We now can see why Vinet could say that all the sublimest thoughts of the profoundest philosophers throughout the ages are not worth, do not counterbalance, one single movement of charity.

I

Love and Time

One must be without conscience and without compassion not to confess that nowadays there is a horrible waste of time, for that time is wasted which, lawfully destined by God to charity and to the relief of human suffering, is diverted from so holy a use. Men try to justify themselves by claiming to have no time. Yet their selfishness has no leisure. Time to do good is never to be merely found; it is charity that must create it. Time is indeed composed not only of hours and minutes but also of love and will. We have little time when we have little love. Like turning to God, beneficence must never be postponed. Charity never says "tomorrow."

Vinet noticed that modern people confuse charity with almsgiving. He found it difficult to believe that such an error is unintentional. For him, it is really an attack upon charity; and charity is Christianity. God demands man rather than some of man's money. There are only two principles for man, both always active and encroaching: selfishness and charity. The one must grow and the other diminish; the one grows only by the spoils of the other. Between these two tendencies which solicit him, man cannot find neutral ground to rest in, he must incline to the one or to the other. Hence it results that, even in not acting, man acts, and that by the very fact that a man does not labor for charity, he does so for selfishness. This explains why simple inaction as regards the afflicted is not only criminal but deteriorating (Matt. 13:12; 25:41–45) and the first punishment that befalls him who leaves good undone is to be less and less capable of doing it. For the authentic Christian, however, the reason, the aim, the object, the interest of life, is charity. The true wealth of life is affection; its true poverty, selfishness. We live in proportion as we love. Egotism is a consumption, a death, a suicide.

A habit of rash and ill-natured judgments shows that the person is not born into the new life—the life of God and charity. Yet indignation is at times as becoming in the Christian as in Jesus himself when he pronounced the terrible words "hypocrites!" and "fools!" Charity therefore sometimes manifests itself through harshness. Meekness may be treachery. There may be love in vehemence and indignation.

Love often brings suffering, but the griefs of charity are a thousand times better than the joys of selfishness; to love is its own reward, its own consolation; always to suffer, yet always to love, would be paradise in comparison with always prospering and always hating. Vulgar happiness consists in receiving, and can never receive enough; love needs to give, and has never given enough; sacrifices exhaust the one, sacrifices sustain the other; and whereas the first would gain nothing in gaining the whole world, the latter enriches itself by its very losses. And when love takes possession of the life of a Christian, that life rises and unfolds itself with the majestic unity of a temple consecrated to the Lord. True love is the foretaste and token of eternal life.

II

BEING IN THE TRUTH

It used to be said of Frederick the Great that, properly speaking, he was not fond of music, but of the flute, and not indeed fond of the flute, but of *his* flute. Most friends of truth love it the same way: that is, just as Frederick loved not music, but *his* music, so too many men love not truth, but *their* truths. Yet truth is not a particular possession of individual men. Truth is, so to speak, an external entity that men must enter. Truth is not an individual subjective interpretation but an objective reality outside the individual. Truth is not a form for Vinet, but a substance, and there is but one way to *know* the truth, namely, to *be in* the truth. Truth is not a mere word or formula: truth is being, life; consequently truth is love, since in the moral world, which is the true, it is love that is life and being, and in this sphere whatever is not love has no existence.

Life is a perpetual birth. And life can no more dispense with symbols than language with metaphors.

God seems to have prepared the truths of human science for his friends and his foes alike. It is not so with religious truths. These God has prepared for them who love him. Not that he has excluded men of genius or learning from their possession; but genius and scholarship do not suffice here as it is with the other sciences. Love is necessary. Love is the only true interpreter of gospel truths. Love renders the truths of the gospel intelligible to man: not indeed those abstract truths which relate to the very essence and being of God, and of which any knowledge is equally inaccessible and useless to us, but those other truths which concern our relation with God, and constitute the very foundation of religion. It is these truths that escape from reason, and are grasped without difficulty by love. And truth comes to us quite alone; brings no extrinsic testimony, invokes no authority but its own, shows itself, and we believe in it as in the light of day, as in our own existence. This has nothing mystical and inconceivable about it. The fact is both natural and supernatural. It is with truth as with those half souls who, according to the idea of an ancient sage, seek their own half in life, recognize it the moment they meet it, and so blend with it as soon as recognized that one can no longer be distinguished from the other. A belief thus formed is never lost, can never be lost, any more than an animated being can lose its instinct; for such a belief has become one of the instincts of the soul. Arguments do not change a man. It is life that teaches life: God that reveals God.

Just as truth is one and indivisible, so the whole truth is to be entered and apprehended only by the whole man. Enter the truth, and you will see from within what cannot be seen from without; practice Christianity and you will know it. To be in the truth is to become, by our affections and conduct, ever more and more like Jesus Christ; it is to follow him spiritually in all the events he has gone through: in his death, by our death to sin; in his resurrection, by our regeneration; in his invisible glory, by our life hid with him in God; in a word, we must spiritually live over again the whole life of Jesus Christ, and this alone can be called knowing the truth and walking in the truth.

Let us not confuse contemplation with observation. The latter is an activity that takes possession of its object, analyzes and dissects it; in contemplation, on the contrary, we might say that it is the object itself that takes possession of man and changes him. Truth (and Vinet speaks here of human truth, of that which makes a man himself to be the truth) is a transformation of the being that receives it. It is not a certain manner of judging; it is the very light of our judgments; it is what constitutes their worth and the worth of the man himself. Truth is order, harmony, peace; it is man restored to the image of God; it is God in man. The truth is God himself. God is the Being of beings, the Idea of ideas, the Truth of truths. Truth is offered by God and may be entered by man. Truth is the thought of God; it is God in the world.

Truth is in God. From the Father of spirits it is communicated in silence and mystery, neither to society nor to the state, but to every spirit which turning to God and humility have prepared to receive it. The secret of the Lord is with them who fear him. Yet truth needs to personify itself in every man. It aims at multiplying itself as many times as there are men to receive the truth. Hence, authentic Christianity is a religion of influence. It is not an institution; it is a virtue; it is a principle of life and impulse implanted in a man. It is a word that, at first, speaks from without, but enters a man and soon becomes an inner word, so that it may be defined as a new soul offered to humanity.

Truth finds itself in actions before it finds itself in ideas; it is in things before it is in words. A thing is true when it is what it ought to be, as a word is true when it says what it ought to say. If therefore a man is not what he ought, it is in vain that he may know the truth, he will not be in the truth—according to the idea of John, who says that by this we know that we are in the truth, if we love our brethren. Truth is the creation of God, consists in the correspondence of all things; now he who does not love, by infringing that general correspondence or harmony which is truth, introduces, so far as it lies in his power, falsehood into the midst of truth. There is therefore no room for drawing a distinction, and saying that man has not love but truth. Not so; if he loves not, he has not truth.

Truth cannot be destroyed. To attack the truth is even a way to announce and spread it. There is no salvation except in the truth. To worship in spirit and in truth is to reproduce faithfully in ourselves the image of him who has loved us. It is not enough merely to abstain from what offends him, but we must, by a principle of love, do whatever is pleasing in his sight, whatever makes us like him. People have a habit of attaching a negative idea to the word "purity." According to the common interpretation, it implies a simple exemption from defilement, the absence of a fault rather than the presence of a quality; but in Christian ethics, purity no more consists in this than does happiness in an exemption from suffering; and just as we are positively happy only insofar as suffering is replaced by enjoyment, so we are only really pure insofar as defects have given place to qualities. Christianity does not consist in not willing; quite the reverse. Christianity simply aims at giving us a will in accordance with that of God, and strengthening it ever more and more in that direction.

The lover of Christian truth knows, however, that there is no victory and no prize except at the end of his course. Yet he who has embraced Jesus Christ by faith, he who in the desert that is this world, has at last found a father, will be both meek and strong in sorrow and misfortune; for what is there at once gentler and stronger than that which combines faith, hope, and love? Do not expect from such a person in the hour of trial either a submission without energy or a proud inflexibility. He is what a man ought to be: armed with courage and adorned with humility, upright before fortune, on his knees before God.

As for the multitude of theories found in circulation today, they are only one more proof of the poverty of principles that characterize modern men. Yet in the number of men and women who do not yet believe, there are some who gravitate toward the truth. There is already something of Christianity in these earnest people who seek everywhere for a God other than the God modern society has made for them. Already they have received from the spirit of God a secret impulse that leads them to seek a God clothed in all the characteristics revealed by the gospel, a God infinitely just, infinitely good—a Providence. Authentic religion holds out her hand, greets them, and waits for the happy moment when, recognizing the striking harmony between Christian revelation and the imperfect revelations of the inner voice, these Christians by anticipation, by desire, by need, shall become Christians also in fact and in profession.

V

The Appropriation of Christianity

I

GOSPEL PENETRATION

IN THIS WORLD everything may be guessed except authentic Christianity; this is not to be penetrated from without, and what Christianity has that is intimate and special is never to be learned from simple hearsay.

The religion of the gospel, Vinet affirms, is not a system of reasoning; it is a force whose property is to invade the heart and to carry along acts. Our religion is neither a rule nor properly a doctrine; it is a relationship that reunites the heart and will of man to the Author of man's being. Religion is not a jargon that one must learn to speak fluently, but a life to be appropriated; and our life must offer to the holy truth a home rather than an echo. It is a life added to our life; it is the life of our very life; it penetrates life from one end to the other as intimately as blood fills the flesh that it nourishes. Christianity, some men say, has given rise to certain additional sentiments in our heart, and additional ideas in our reason; Vinet says, rather, that Christianity has given us a new heart and a new reason. In this intrinsic, inner proof are found both the evidence of Christianity and an authority greater than all external testimonies: yes, truth has its evidence in itself, and when we would provide ourselves with external proofs in order to believe the truth, it is, as if we would light a candle to see the sun.

The decisive argument for the gospel therefore does not consist in the form (historicity of Jesus' miracles, fulfillment of the prophecies, etc.) but in an intuition, the orientation of which is neither rational nor mystical, but religious and ethical. Vinet distrusts vague mysticism, for it may lead to disobedience, while religion is, first of all, complying with God's will.

On the other hand, Vinet has no confidence in intellectualism: Christianity is mysterious in proportion to its sublimity. The expectation of penetrating rationally the mystery of Christianity results from a false understanding of the role of reason in matters of religion. In the appropriation of Christianity, reasonings have not the first place. God has sent his message of deliverance to the heart. Love can be understood only by love. Like Pascal and the Jansenist Saint-Cyran, Vinet does not postulate an absolute incompatibility between reason and the faith of the heart. He simply inverts the order established by the unbelief of the will. What Pascal and Vinet call the "heart" has the first rank, the principal mission, priority. From the heart, reason must receive light: first love and you shall know later on.

As with Pascal, the problem is man himself in all his impulses and conflicts, responses and contradictions. Vinet finds the answer in Christ and God, for even ethics can possess its truth and rightness only in the thought of God. Only in giving ourselves to him is there free and clear moral energy. Separated from the thought of God, conscience is in our nature only a whim, an enigma, a nonsense. Thus, the gospel is the conscience of the conscience itself and Christianity is the conscience itself exalted to its ultimate degree of strength. Christianity is a fact of conscience as well as a fact of revelation. And revealed truth is a thousand times higher than common sense.

II

FAITH AND ETHICS

In the age preceding Vinet, the teaching of Christian doctrine was entirely separate from that of Christian morals. The early Awakening of his time had been a testimony to the indissoluble union of Evangelical dogma and ethics, which was one of the reasons for its success. Since 1823 Vinet's attention fell upon this problem. He conceived the germ of a solution that he perfected by bringing closer and closer the doctrinal element and the practical element of Christianity till he joined and identified them through his idea of faith. Faith is the means through which we embrace the religion of the Crucified One. The appropriation of Christianity is the principal topic Vinet preaches. His concept of faith, subtle and delicate though it appears, is indeed of the highest importance. For it really underlies and conditions both the apologetics and ethics of the Swiss thinker, and explains his whole methodology.

Faith consists in believing, and believing is to hold a thing true and certain. This, however, is only the beginning, the minimum of faith. For true faith is a noble exercise of all the human faculties: the heart, the conscience, and the intellect. If we subtract one of these factors from faith, it is true faith no longer: if the heart be won without the conscience and reason, faith is only a sensibility irritated by formidable images or flattered by seductive fancies; if conscience alone be followed, we have the religion of regrets, not that of faith, hope, and love; if reason only be called forth, we have a mere philosophy without influence on our inner life. Hence faith is that direction or movement which carries *the whole of man* toward the object of his religion. It is a man's total response to God's revelation in Christ.

The object of Christianity is indeed not an abstract dogma, not a theory of the world origins, not a book; it is a fact, a person, it is Jesus Christ and him crucified. This fact, this Person, offers himself naturally to the glance before the thought; and that which acts upon us is this object itself. We do not believe in Christendom. We believe in Jesus Christ. Whatever Christian action there is in this world, it is the work not of Christendom, which is itself only an effect, but of Christ. The true relations in which we stand as Christians are not intellectual,

not relations between our minds and an abstraction, but relations of one Person with another person. The Object of our
faith is invisible, but not impersonal: we do not converse with
him as with an idea or ideal, that is to say, as with ourselves,
but as with a Being who is actually with us always, even to
the end of the world.

Faith, far from being a mere simple event foreign to our
will is, on the contrary, the most real and important use we
can make of our liberty, for it consists essentially in successively
accepting the verdict that declares us all to be fallen and
condemned, and the amnesty that raises us by humbling us;
faith is an abdication of our own righteousness, a voluntary
homage to the holiness of God, a consecration of our whole life
to his service; in a word, faith is the most energetic as well as
the most decisive, the most moral as well as the most happy
act of which the grace of God can render us capable; and it is
just by rendering us capable of this act *par excellence* that God
saves us. This act, destined to place us in communication of
thought, will, and practice with Christ, is a moral act: Faith
is a desire, a homage, a promise, almost a love. It is all these
at once, and it is the most simple of all things: a look, a gaze of
the heart toward the God of mercy, "an earnest and vehement
consideration of Jesus Christ crucified," the abandonment of all
our interests into his hands, the repose of the heart and peace
of mind in the certainty of his love and power—such is faith.
Intellect knows: to know is to classify; but the soul sees: to
see is to penetrate. In the intimacy of the fact, it is not to
classify, it is to name!

Faith is both to give up and to take possession, an act of
abandonment and of reception. Faith is essentially to receive
Jesus, to retain him, evermore to be united with him by that
mysterious insertion which grafts us as many shoots into the
vinestock that is Christ, from whom, by virtue of this union, we
henceforth derive all our vital force and whose life becomes
ours. "Whose life becomes ours!" Yes, and not only his life but
also his death and his resurrection. The facts of the gospel, the

dogma, thus contemplated by the believer, are transfused into his own life, so that in the Christian religion all is related to life: none of its teachings remains "idle," none stands by itself and without determining man's conduct.

Faith consists in receiving into the heart things proper to change it. Hence this faith, which God gives after having given its object, does what without it no work could have done or can ever do: it justifies us, it clothes us with the only goodness of which we are capable, that of repentance, the abandonment of self-righteousness, hope in God alone; and the surrender into his hands of all our pretensions and presumptions. It empties and purifies the vessel of our heart, renders it meet to receive God, and becomes the wholesome and vigorous root of a new life, since not only does it submit us to God by the most absolute self-abdication but it unites us to him by the most absolute trust. Faith is a faculty or function; now action is the sign of a faculty; the *faculty* that does nothing is not a faculty. Our faith, one with our works, manifests itself in them, or, to use the words of James, it acts *with our works,* which on their part render it perfect, or consummate it. Faith and works, the trunk and the branches, form a whole, one only work, one only righteousness; but sometimes we are said to be saved by faith, because the principle includes the whole; at other times we are said to receive according to our works, because what we do is the evidence and the *measure* of what we are. The measure of faith is for each one of us the measure of peace, charity, liberty, life. James and Paul combat opposite errors in one same spirit, and confront two forms of Pharisaism: Paul that of the law, James that of faith. If faith saves, it is because it produces hope and charity; the faith that does not produce these is not faith.

The Christian therefore is not a man who has expelled one theory from his mind to make room for another theory; he is a man who nourishes himself with the promises of God as his only hope; who incessantly strips off all pretensions of his own; who offers himself daily as a sacrifice to his Savior, and no longer lives for himself, but lets Christ live in him, and determines that the life which he must still live in the flesh shall be lived by faith in the Son of God, who has loved him.

Such an adherence to the truth of Christianity necessarily involves a revolution in us, and, so to speak, a displacement of the basis upon which we had been accustomed to rest our judgments. This displacement of the center of gravity in our life is an invisible revolution, says Vinet, a mysterious transmutation. The authentic Christian obeys God because he loves God; and he loves God because he is loved by God. There is indeed nothing but the love of God that can conquer the hardness of man's heart. Man must believe that God loves him and man will believe this by believing in an infinite love. Man will not understand eternal life if he does not understand that it begins here and now and dates from the moment in which God taught him to love him.

Salvation is thus, in the life of a man, a great crisis. Conversion is the movement that turns a man from one side to the other, from the dark and gloomy west toward the east, from which light breaks forth. The Christian faith coming into a man is such an event that it can be but the gift of God.

Yet, Vinet writes, that which characterizes a Christian man is not exactly enthusiasm and ardor; still less is it talent and eloquence; it is humble faith—faith that knows how to wait; it is humility before God; it is, above all, love. Christianity is but ethics growing in a soil alimented by the grace of God. Salvation therefore is not a material, external fact; salvation is not without, but within. It is inward deliverance. It is a state of the soul. The gospel is a force, a virtue that transforms those who study it. Christianity is creative life: "The gospel associates itself with everything; it purifies, corrects, and reorganizes everything; it reconstructs within its own sphere a world where there is scope enough for all our faculties, aliment for all our powers, horizon for all our thoughts." This may seem foolish, but a religion that appears reasonable to all the world could not be the true religion. If there were no obscurities in Christianity, the heart would leave all to be done by the mind. The mind then would suffice for all; and the heart, thenceforth having no part in the search after truth, would leave man to stand about mournfully in the midst of those empty and abstract notions which men call philosophy. What Vinet denies is the competence of human reason, destitute of the help of revelation, to throw light on the great question of our destiny, and to reestablish unity in our inner life. Arguments do not change the man. Conclusions at which we have arrived by a series of logical deductions will hardly produce upon the mind the impression of reality. There will always be a great difference between arguing and seeing, between concluding and experiencing. This force, which supplies the place of evidence in religious matters, is *faith*. It is true that by ourselves, and without God, we can no more repent than we can believe, obey, persevere; but God gives this faith: it is life that teaches life; God that reveals God.

Thus, by nature, faith is experimental rather than authoritarian. Hence result the free, bold, and sure words of spiritual religion: "Truth, without the research of the truth, is but half the truth. One believes well only after having doubted." For one has found that truth is not formal thought but, so to speak, a substance; hence again "there is but one way to know the truth; it is to be *in* the truth."

From the very character of Christianity it is clear that true faith is individual and subjective. It is individual: it is by immediate relationship with Christ that man is restored; and "the truth demands to personalize itself in each man." Faith, moreover, is subjective: it consists in receiving in the heart things proper to change it. Faith is a life.

But here Vinet makes the most important reservation: faith is true, ethical, and efficient only if it has the right and proper object. Faith without the object of faith is nothing. It may even be an evil. For it is to its object, Vinet says, that faith owes its character and effects. It is not in the measure of how much we believe, but according to what and in whom we believe that we become all we can and all we ought to be. The object of the

Christian faith is Christ. Only by looking to Christ do we come to understand the secret of life; otherwise everything remains enigmatic for us. Only by following Christ with childlike confidence is our existence restored to true life. Only thus are we enabled to follow the impulses from above and to execute the divine inspirations. This obedience, however, is far from being slavish or resulting from constraint. Our obedience is spontaneous and joyful, because it is the fruit of love. The true poverty of life is selfishness; its true wealth is love. Our religion is not a religion of detachment, for then it would not be religion; our religion is a religion of attachment, that is, of love.

As a transitory conclusion, may we say with G. Frommel that Vinet's solution of the problem of the relation of doctrine and ethics in Christianity is but the consistent development of his apologetics. If man, indeed, recognizes the truth of Christianity by its response to the vital needs of man, and if the condition of such a recognition is an earnest contemplation of the person of Christ, what else and more could the believer do? He will more and more make Christ the object of a "vehement consideration." "Looking at" means believing; and "believing" means receiving in ourselves the object of our faith and love. Faith and dogma have the same object, that is, Christ and his life. And what other result would we have in receiving by faith this object than to live by it and thus to transcribe the historical facts of the gospel into our inward and outward life? So, through faith, the events, facts, doctrine, and dogma found in the Gospels are actually put in operation and thus become ethics, that is to say, Christian action.

By resolving through an intelligent and practical mysticism the apparent dualism of morals and doctrine, Vinet the theologian consummates the apologist. Since the transcendent substance of the dogma, namely, the person and work of Christ, may be and is transposed and reproduced in the life of the Christian, how could we still doubt that man is made for the gospel and the gospel for man? That the gospel is the truth? When a man has entered the truth, he knows the truth. And the truth itself becomes personalized in that man. The evidence is irrefutably given, since fellowship with the living Christ is a moral contact whose fruits are justice, peace, joy, and love, which are, in turn, the Evangelical concept of deliverance and salvation. Our joy especially honors God. The gospel can thus be incarnated in the concrete reality of human beings. And the authentic Christian evidences this in the world of men. "A true Christian is a complete vindication of Christianity."

VI

An Estimate of
Modern Civilization

I
THE MODERN BABEL

VINET IS REPORTED to have said, in 1837, that "barbarians are coming not from the North but from below our feet." By these new barbarians he meant the masses to which democracy in Europe had entrusted the decision of the most delicate political and international questions. Since, for Vinet, majorities were fatally bound to be mediocrities, government by the European masses would open a new period of history ruled by Caesars coming neither from the old nobility nor from the middle classes, which in Vinet's time still held the power, but from below. From the lower classes several new Caesars or masterminds of our twentieth century such as Mussolini and Hitler have come indeed, with the result that is evident to us all. Living in a time of agitation and revolutions for equality, Vinet regretted that the fact of the corruption of the human heart was forgotten and that laws, charters, and constitutions were conferring political and social rights without discrimination—as if it were to angels and without even the mention of duties. Giving away rights without insisting on duties would fatally impoverish society as a whole. A Christian, Vinet wrote, knows his own civil rights under the name of *functions;* it is the rights of others that it behooves him to know as *rights.* It is this principle of life and health that modern democracy lacks.

Political life can no more be guaranteed by charters than confidence between individuals can advantageously be replaced by contracts—written, signed, and sealed. On the contrary, these charters, like all contracts, prove that mutual trust or confidence does not exist among men. Charters are but the provisional props of an insecure building without foundations. Public education, moreover, by offering prizes and sponsoring competition, has placed ambition at the head or rather in the place of all motives that may act upon young people. Public education undisguisedly substitutes self-love for love; hence vanity has become the basis of the moral life of a whole new generation. As a consequence, nowadays goodwill, generosity, and love are impossible. Now, the man who loves neither God nor his neighbor is in exile, a voluntary prisoner of himself. Selfishness is absolute loneliness.

This new social and political system, writes Vinet, is a permanent conspiracy against our individuality; and nothing more threatens our inner liberty than the outer "organized liberty" in which we live and in which we participate. Today there are no longer individualities, but only masses. In our modern society we are born originals and we die copies. Modern life, by taking us out of ourselves with distractions and incessantly blending us with the masses, renders our life more superficial in proportion as it extends and diffuses it. The thinking necessary to conviction is hardly possible in the public parade wherein we live.

A society where individuality is proscribed and made impossible may be socialist, but cannot be sociable, cannot be human, cannot be living. In short, it cannot be a society at all. Individuality is the basis of our proper worth, for, in order to be anything, we must begin by *being;* in other words, our qualities must be our own. In this sense individuality is rare. Most men, instead of living at home, live, as it were, in other people's dwellings. That is to say, they have a lease of, they have rented, their opinions and their morality. Every man does not have an individuality, although in the present society every man must be an individual. In modern life, one is not oneself from the first; one becomes so only by an act of will. The question is how to get down to our real self through the successive layers (formed by the ideas of others or of the community at large) with which our own self is always thickly covered. It is as with the drilling of an artesian well, answers Vinet: these layers have to be bored through, so as to get to self-discovery. We must find the real self or *me*. If you wish the living waters to gush out, be *yourselves:* determine and circumscribe your position; have a focus (*foyer*); be yourself—this is your first duty. A real individuality has not two editions.

By their nature emotional and intolerant, the masses will sponsor neither liberal laws nor generous measures. When liberty is something else than simply a means of moral progress, all is lost in politics. Vinet sees nothing in common between the masses as such and the truth. Truth cannot present itself, cannot dwell except in the individual man or woman, inasmuch as the individual alone is organized to perceive the truth. Unless the enormous paradox of numbers making truth be admitted, the opinion of a whole nation could no more be rendered authoritative on a single individual than can the opinion of a single individual upon a whole people. One, two, ten, a thousand men, many millions of men—Vinet sees no relationship between numbers as such and truth. As for him, he says that truth is in God. From him it is given in silence and mystery, not to the masses, not to the nation, but to any man or woman whom God sees to be fit to receive it.

Vinet was rather pessimistic about the outcome of our celebrated modern civilization. Several times he called our modern world of men a Second Babel and a Confusion of Tongues. Civilization, in its etymological sense, is the formation of the citizen, of the complete man; but as understood today, it is the progress of the intellect in the interests of material progress and physical well-being. Science has not created this strange situation; but science—which always follows in the train of morals, and models itself upon the mores of the community—faithfully represents this idea. It has put psychology in the place of morality, and utility in the place of rightness. Only touching the intellect and unable to reach the man himself, modern science has simply created better tools to be sold for the sake of money and used for both good and evil. Modern wars are a clear illustration as to how these tools can be used. "A whole nation," says Vinet, "may fall to be the dupe of a coarse sophism, and in such people the man of the most enlightened and stable mind is nationally considered to be a fool." Entire nations are carried away by strange forces. "Nothing is so terrible as logic in irrationality."

Ignoring antiquity, modern man thinks himself better. He claims and shows forth his higher standards of living, better communications, better housing, and greater comforts. Material goods, says Vinet, do not constitute progress and if modern industry be pursued in another spirit than the spirit of charity and justice, there may be gain and profit, but there cannot be true progress. Mankind seems to forget that the first inventions, the first "progress," in the current sense of the word, occurred in the family of Cain the assassin. So long as progress of the human heart or inner man does not correspond to the progress of arts and sciences, progress will always be an object of alarm. As ultimately there are but two realities: God himself and the thought of God in man, nothing is progress in God's eyes except what restores the image of God in humanity. Vinet the Christian, who sees all in God's light, gives the name of progress to nothing else. It is only with very decided reservations that Vinet believes that man's perfectibility is possible. The renewal of things could come only from a renewal of men who make them.

Christianity might have attracted a few individuals and through them influenced others, but it has not fashioned our social body. Modern civilization has not radically influenced the heart of man. Our civilization is not deep; its action is superficial. It encloses man's passions in a net, but it does not kill them. It covers the savage without affecting his inner core. Etymologically from the Latin verb *librare* (to weigh, to appreciate), liberty would be the ability and the right to ponder, to appreciate by and of ourselves, and to choose. The modern industry and system, by destroying personal thought, makes any "pondering" and meditation impossible. As for "choosing," materialism, that is, the love of material goods, leans with all its weight toward tyranny. What today endangers freedom is not, as of old, superstition. It is anxiety, the passion for gain and well-being in the sense of ever higher standards of physical life. It leads to Caesarism. Since the actions of a Caesar are generally irrational and arbitrary, tyranny is the sovereign disorder. Death is the true name of unity without liberty.

II

SOCIALISM AND INDIVIDUALISM

Especially toward the end of his life Vinet more than once wrote about socialism. He had no high regard for contemporary socialist or communist movements born of envy for others' property and greed for material goods. Yet he said that the socialist or social point of view is contained in Christianity, and is a point to which the friends of religious progress should turn their attention.

In his opinion, the socialist idea as currently found in the world is a very ancient one: on it rested the whole classical and pagan world. Its funeral knell was sounded by Christianity. The sentiment of individuality, or the principle of personal liberty, sprang from the gospel. Under the inspiration of Paul it asserted itself and flourished. It then found a point of support in the feeling of personal independence that characterized the ancient German peoples. But the antique socialist idea took refuge in Roman Catholicism, which is to socialism what the species is to the genus. The new Rome insensibly inaugurated a new socialism. Catholicism for Vinet is nothing else. After many attempts, in the beginning of the sixteenth century, authority rediscovered its basis in God and his law. The principle of individuality received from our Protestant Reformers, not an explicit consecration, but irrevocable pledges.

The Reformation in the abstract is, for some, room for religion, for others, a protest; but in truth it was at its birth even better than a reform. As the Reformation established the right, even the duty, of depending in life only on God, it was the reintegration of the moral (inward) element in religion. The Reformation was a revolution and a restoration: it is so still, it will ever be so for some men by the very circumstance that it has restored all responsibility to individuality, and, by removing it from the convenient regime of resting on external authority, it imposes on men the severest of all laws—the perfect law of liberty of which James (ch. 1:25) speaks. Be not deceived, those who dislike Protestantism most, hate not its freedom but its rigor. The severity and earnestness of its thought are no less a grievance than the boundless career that the Reformation seems to have opened out to liberty of thought.

Nevertheless, pagan socialism was not defeated, because it survives in the very pale of Protestantism under the form of national religion. And there is nowhere so much narrowness as in national sects and national denominations. For Vinet, nationalism is simply collective egotism—a hydra-headed monster. The nation is not our end or purpose, and ought not to be. The nation is too narrow to circumscribe the whole man. The whole man finds room for himself only in God. The gospel does not need to protest against nationalism, for the gospel is that very protestation.

All nationalists are unconsciously socialists; all socialists are unwittingly nationalists. In good logic, a socialist state is either a barracks or a monastery, according to the ethics and temperament of the nation. For Vinet, the socialist state is necessarily communist in this sense: that it is theoretically the single proprietor of all things, and the individuals are reduced to using things temporarily in proportion as the individuals are useful to the state. Such a state would impose upon all its own religion, its taste, and its philosophy if it had one. By placing man under eternal tutelage, this sort of socialism implicitly presupposes the degradation of human nature and the impossibility of its restoration. If even by a miracle socialism could have made all necessary offices attractive, it would have made of man a "thinking stomach." If this be the last word of progress, says Vinet, let us, rather, regress!

If a man dreads that kind of system, he must as far as possible maintain in all its integrity and in all its bearings the principle of religious liberty that is preeminently that of individuality, and consequently the correction of a profane socialism. Vinet therefore affirms political liberalism against a socialism that sacrifices man to things. His liberalism, however, is to guarantee, not investments and riches, but moral man. Liberty and goodness require a religious foundation or principle. All social truths are in the same case: religious truth is the only firm basis for any of them, because the sentiment of obligation, the conscience, is the root of all true liberty and morality. But, some will say, is not this individualism? Vinet answers: Individualism (*individualisme*) is not individuality (*individualité*). Individualism and individuality are two sworn enemies. Individualism is the obstacle, yes, even the negation of society. Individuality is that to which society owes all its savor, life, and reality. Nowhere does individualism prosper more easily than where there is an absence of individuality, and there is no more atomistic policy than that of despotism.

Although the thought of the individual man cannot form itself outside society or without its help, it is the individual person, not society, that thinks, feels, hopes, believes, and loves. Individuality does not consist in mere differing from other men, but in realizing under an individual form, and therefore more energetically, the general characteristics of humanness. To be an individuality is to be as much as possible the proprietor of one's opinions, one's feelings, in short, one's whole self, instead of being only their tenant—the condition to which many of the most learned and famous men of today have chosen to reduce themselves. Individuality is the principle and the beginning of a vast and living unity.

Democracy, regarded in our day as the normal, definitive,

and ultimate condition of society, is, for Vinet, perhaps only an important crisis, a state of transition that society has to go through. The current and common epithet "Christian" as applied to present democracy does not alter the case; in such a combination of words the substantive (democracy) chooses its adjective (Christian) but remains what it is. Vinet well knows that Thucydides twenty-three hundred years ago defined democracy in these terms: "As our government is not in the hands of a small number of citizens, but in the hands of the majority, it has received the name of democracy." Yet for Vinet a certain thing desired by the greatest number is neither just nor social by that fact alone. On the contrary, it may be execrable and subversive of all society in the true sense of the word; and were it the will of all against one, it ought not to be done.

Vinet no more understands the divine right of all than the divine right of one. The right is God in us; the useful is the ego of each one of us. Ego sets up interest as the only master of man and human life. The useful has become nowadays the criterion of the true. The monopoly of power by the middle class would bequeath no great result to history; according to Vinet, a purely commercial republic would produce only commercial results. The new modern age has for its religion pantheism; for its politics, the sovereignty or rather the divinity of the people; for its conscious or unconscious social theory, communism; for its political economics, phalansterianism. Its morality is not yet invented, for morality would have no part in this new system, anyhow. History as a whole is a chain that man drags along the ground so long as it be not connected with its first link, the ring riveted in the Rock of Ages.

III

THEOCRACY

To Vinet, Jesus Christ is like a mountain from the top of which the eye takes in the whole extent of the country and reaches to its utmost limits. Not only out of religious conviction, but also through observing that modern society is not properly a product of sociability, Vinet came to see more and more clearly that, strictly speaking, there is no true system of thought except theocracy.

Under the empire of the living God, an order whose secret is beyond our present understanding may be confidently hoped, certainly foreseen, enjoyed beforehand; for such an order already exists, perfect and entire, in the very fact that God is and reigns. Theocracy therefore is not a system of political organization, but a fact, and not even an ordinary fact, but a miracle. Christianity in its vital and characteristic elements is always a stranger in this world and an intruder in our society. The gospel addresses itself to individual men. It is not to an abstract negative man, neutralized by the ideas of all other men, that the gospel addresses its message; it is to you, to me, to him, to her, to each and every one of us, just as nature has made us. It is to each man immediately that God has said in his gospel, "Come, let us reason together!" (Isa. 1:18). Each man is taken by himself with what he has that is peculiar and exclusive. No collective being interposes between him and God: no national or secular idea answers in his name to the divine interrogation. It deals with him alone and exclusively, as if he were the only one in the world, as though he were humanity. There is no system; there is only the revelation of God, which can at the same time, and by the same means, snatch us from individualism and consecrate our individuality.

Out of love for all men, God has willed that men should form society. He has ordained for these beings the arrangement that suited them best; but he has not created the beings for the arrangement. He, the all-wise God, has seen and declared that it is not good for man to be alone. Consequently, God has co-ordained man for man, has decreed that man should be man only by that contact, has rendered society as essential to man as his heart or brain, has willed him, conceived him as associated; so God has made man essentially social, causing man's character to depend upon that of a member of the community. Man enters in the world as subject to the law of solidarity, and society is to be to man what the soil is to the plant. The importance of society is great; but this importance of society (being entirely relative to individuality) is only the individual's own importance under a different name. Vinet imagines society as a being, yet he also realizes that society has no existence apart from the individual—nay, it exists in that individual as a tendency, as an attribute. Society is man seeking his fellowman. Yet we are fit for social life upon condition of having a life of our own, and we truly belong to society on condition of being, in the first place, completely men.

In order not to be mixed up with rugged individualists, as the reader recalls, Vinet called the ensemble of his social views "individuality" (*individualité*). He carefully distinguished it from individualism (*individualisme*), and, against the socialists, added squarely that his thought or vision represented the true interests of society, while he considered the real enemies of the social body to be those men who deify their nation, lend themselves by their silence to a false conventional uniformity, and render to Caesar (that is, to society) that which belongs only to God. A society where individuality is proscribed or made practically impossible may be socialist, but cannot be sociable, cannot be a society, cannot in short be human at all because it contradicts the design of the living God and robs him of his own—which is man.

Vinet's thought in social matters is not a system and an end in itself but a means and a method. The end, after all, is society itself; the aim is its greater good. Hence Vinet's position is favorable to society. It aims through individual enrichment to bring life and strength to the human community. The contrary tendency, absolutism or Caesarism (Vinet regards Louis XIV as the great teacher of our modern utopists), impoverishes society to that degree to which it robs the individuality and, by substituting a will foreign to the will of men, fatally leads man to debasement and immorality; theocracy (as conceived by Vinet) promotes man to moral maturity by calling him to be a free servant and friend of God through a living faith and a personal will. Hence, Vinet's deep love for liberty: "As long as I live, I will be true to the cause of freedom. Liberty is the one way to unity. Even though liberty were fraught with all imaginable perils, while slavery promised all tranquility, I would still prefer liberty. For, liberty is life, and slavery death. But separate the idea of liberty from that of its purpose (which is our individual perfecting, the good of society, and the glory of God) and what is left under the name of liberty? Nothing but a savage instinct!" The cross of Christ overthrows the human ego. Yet the potentially overthrown ego reasserts itself in man, insists on rearing itself again, and rises the higher the lower it has been cast down.

IV

WITH JOY AND TREMBLING

Vinet therefore emphasizes the importance of the indissoluble bonds that tie every individual to the human race. Vinet was one of the first to call attention to the fact of solidarity. Mankind is a solid, a whole; and man is a solid with mankind. Man is "solidary": he comes into this world under the law of solidarity. That is, there exists a mutual dependence between men, so that some cannot be happy or perfected unless the others also are so. Not only by entering life does each of us reap the inheritance of all past centuries (such a rich legacy that whatever we might contribute in our turn, we always die being insolvent debtors) but we are human only on that condition. Each man exists because of social efforts anterior to him; hence he is under obligation to contribute in his turn to the common good. Only to the animal has it been given to suffice to itself, says Vinet. God has coordinated man with man; he wished that man might become man only through this contact.

Vinet, on the other hand, insists that collective entities are but abstractions and that in order to refashion society, the individuals composing it should first be formed anew. The divine freedom awakens the human. To become Christians, we must first of all be ourselves. To make Christians, God wishes first of all to find men. Liberty is the capacity to ponder and to choose. God is the protector of liberty (Jer. 34:8–22). Wherever it will be desired to give free course to true democracy, it will be necessary to give free course to true religion. Christianity is the immortal seed of freedom in the world. At the same time, the gospel is the most social among systems; therefore let it inspire the morals and let its spirit dictate the laws. If Protestants are to rejoice in the restoration of the gospel through the Reformation and with it the restitution of liberty and personal responsibility, they must do so with trembling.

According to Vinet, religious conviction is the inward assurance that God has spoken, and the sentiment of a mysterious fellowship between the Creator and his creature. It is impossible that this sentiment should not give rise to a profound joy, and it is equally impossible that this joy should not be mixed with trembling. Vinet professed to be suspicious of a religion which, while alleging that God has come down to man (an essential characteristic of the true religion), would put man at ease with the Eternal Lord by suppressing that trembling. The prophets and the apostles, Vinet says, regarded that trembling as a symptom of religious joy. True religion, according to Vinet, ever increases both the trembling and the joy within man.

But there are still other reasons why Christian joy and gratitude are, in modern men, mixed with trembling. Our huge modern structure and collective life are frail. Civilization represses, or better, compresses, man's passions and greed; it does not suppress them. Modern civilization is like a suit put on a savage: the new clothes neither changed nor did away with him. The savage, the man of nature, is ready to reappear whenever the occasion offers or the temptation is presented. Civilization has not absorbed the brutal element in man, the *pars leonina* of which Horace speaks. Civilization renders its explosions less frequent but more terrible; it stops up the ways of egress; it rolls a stone to the mouth of the cave of Cacus; but the ancient giant and brigand Cacus is still there. And at any time Cacus may come out of his den stronger than ever.

As a Christian, Vinet thinks therefore that the only basic and real perfecting of man depends upon the pure sovereignty of God. So long as the individual expects a judgment beyond and above this world, he is greater than society, which expects none. Christianity ought to counterbalance old Cacus and become a regulator of all social and human relations. As Christians see in the family the symbol of the Kingdom of God, it is in the spirit of a true family that society should be reconstituted. Christians are not first equals and then brothers. They are first made brothers in Christ, and then because they are brothers in the eyes of God, they are equals.

In Vinet's views, the true interests of society and those of true religion are closely united. A wholesome spiritualism favors liberty; true and sound political liberalism is spiritual. Materialism, that is, the love of material goods, on the contrary, leads men to Caesarism and tyranny. Uniformity is the seal of fiction and falsehood. Uniformity is a symptom of death. There is true unity only where diversity is possible. A soul has to be restored to modern man who no longer has one. True Christianity is the most powerful reactive against a false uniformity. Christianity is both, and alternatively, a solvent and a cement of society.

The gospel did not invent morality. Some of its finest sayings had long before been in circulation: the gospel did not so much promulgate as it did establish these maxims upon a new basis, and quicken them with a new spirit; and the prerogative of the divine word is not so much that of announcing a new morality as of giving power to practice the old. If the true social unity be the harmony of thoughts and the concurrence of wills, society will be strong and real in proportion to the presence of thought and will in each of its members. Often Vinet separated, but in order to reunite: what he calls individuality should lead us to social love; Protestantism should bring us to true catholicity; liberty to unity. Vinet the Christian wishes each man to be inwardly rich in order that the common treasury of humanity may become rich. Christianity alone works seriously for the good of man. For Vinet the humanist, freedom is the foundation of moral life; it is but a correlative of that conscience which condemns whatever we do against our inner conviction. It is freedom that gives a moral character to our deeds: a will unable to choose ceases to be responsible; hence, if a will is compelled from outside to do an action, this act, even if good in itself, has no moral significance. Man is subject to an inner law that calls him to exercise his highest functions, or faculties, and thereby to fulfill a truly divine vocation. Man ought to accomplish this law in every direction. Only freedom can make the obedience and the accomplishment of this law outwardly possible and inwardly moral. Only voluntary, free, and intelligent goodness is true goodness.

Vinet desired human society to attain a higher goal than mere material prosperity. He dreamed of a Christian society that would assure for each of its members the possibility of flourishing and unfolding all his spiritual possibilities and thus becoming a real person. It is as a whole that the gospel is extraordinary. The spirit of the gospel is a new spirit. As it creates new men, so it ought to create a new society.

CHAPTER

VII

Art and Literature

ACCORDING TO VINET, modern idolatry has raised two altars to which a crowd of idolaters press forward. One of these is the altar erected to matter. The other altar is that erected to intellect. Upon both, human victims are offered, for all idolatrous worship, says Vinet, is murderous worship. It is clear that a man's greed does not hesitate to murder indirectly other men for the sake of profit; and to gain, he sacrifices even himself. Yet the adoration of intellect has its barbarity as well as the adoration of matter. The intellectual man, too, in order to succeed, spares nothing and nobody. And nowadays he who despises others most too often passes for having the most sagacity. The heart often has intellect, but the intellect has no heart.

Respectable men now question the truth of Christianity and reduce it to a mere *possibility*. Vinet thanks these intellectuals for having supplied an expression so fortunate and so well suited to sum up his thought. For, if in their minds this word "possible" is not synonymous with "impossible," if they give to this word its true meaning of "that can exist," it expresses, according to Vinet, the normal condition of Christianity in this world. Just as the preservation of man is a creation perpetually renewed, so the existence of Christianity on earth is a perpetual birth. It is with Christianity as with its head Jesus Christ. The eternal Christ says: "Verily, verily, I say unto you, Except a corn of wheat fall into the ground and die, it abideth alone: but if it die, it bringeth forth much fruit." (John 12:24.)

85

To die incessantly that it may incessantly be renewed: such
is the law presiding over Christianity; such is its force. To die,
that is to say, to separate itself continually from every power
that proceeds not from its own principle, to renounce in anticipation and at every moment the empire of this world, to live
only of its own life, and to receive it day by day, and hour by
hour, and minute by minute, from Him from whom life
emanates: such is the law of Christianity, such is its strength.
Christianity is possible; it is, then, true that this immaterial
substance, this breath, this spirit, exists of itself; it is, then, true
that Christianity, a thought, a simple thought, will transcend
the ages, will be present at the revolutions of empires, and will
never quit the world till the world shall be no longer.

The intellect has to deal only with ideas. As it has no call
to exercise charity, it is the inner man who is bound to be
charitable. The mind is skillful in dividing; the thoughts that
unite individualities spring from the heart. The spirit of the
gospel gives this new spirit. It creates a different man. Each
profession, each art, should be exercised in a Christian spirit.
Even the statesman should be a Christian. If God makes use of
means, we may well make use of them. Our faculties are not
more unworthy of us than we are unworthy of God. Let us
therefore place all these means, that is, the whole man, at
God's service.

Now, man comprehends art. Man is essentially an artist.
Take away art, and man is no longer man. Art therefore ought
to be dedicated to God and to the new man. The most minute
details of life ought to be influenced by Christianity, which has
a hand as delicate as it is powerful. The new man therefore
ought to be an accomplished man. Vinet himself intimately
knew the whole classic Greek, Latin, Italian, German, French,
and English literature. His keen Christianity made him one of
the great Christian humanists. If a French senator, Edmond de
Pressensé, called him "the pastor of his thoughts," another
French senator, E. Schérer, paid Vinet this tribute: "Vinet lived
the life of his century most completely, and from the heights of

his intellectual position he spoke the language of the gospel to the world, and the language of the world to the church. Just to have seen him was a light and a call; to have known him is a blessing for which we are grateful to God."

I

VINET, LITERARY CRITIC

Vinet brought into the republic of letters a new tone: an austere conscience, hence lofty moral principles, and, above all, a warm Christianity—expressed through a delicacy of thought and an aesthetic sensitivity that remind us of Greek refinement. At the University of Basel (which made Vinet a doctor in 1826) and at the Lausanne Academy, Vinet lectured on the whole of French literature. In his thirty-sixth work on the history of Romanticism Ernest Seillière has brought to light the splendid achievements of Vinet as a Christian historian and man of letters. Vinet's numerous articles, book reviews, literary works, and wide correspondence with men of letters establish him as the most distinguished humanist and literary critic in French-speaking Protestantism. Vinet is remarkable for his psychological interest. His method has been called a living psychology. Several characteristic traits of Vinet have either determined or colored the whole of French Protestant thought. Though Vinet had not given a systematic form to his views, and maybe for this reason, all the different tendencies in the Protestantism of France and western Switzerland drew inspirations from Vinet. All these schools of thought felt the necessity of being, if not in full harmony, then certainly not in contradiction with him. Calvin and Vinet are indeed the two great representatives of their Protestantism.

Literature has everywhere preceded literary theories; the fact has forerun the idea. And Vinet's ideas are as follows: Literature is the beautiful realized by language. Literature embraces all those writings in which man synthetically reveals himself to man. Hence literature is truly related to the knowledge of

human life. In every product of human literature Vinet finds
the evidence of a particular state of society. Though not aiming
at a history of morals, Vinet draws from literature data for
ethics. And ethics he defines as the art of living. The purpose
of ethics is finding principles lofty and mighty enough to domi-
nate our existence so as to create affection, and through affection a better life. Man is indeed determined ultimately by his
affections. An affection can be overcome only by another
affection.

Until the day when man will finally seek on high his point
of reference and find in God the fixed principle of his existence,
all the human systems can be reduced to four or five principal
ideas that follow one another throughout the ages of the world.
These ideas always come back under different aspects and various names. Man by himself alone has found only parts of the
truth, yet man never was entirely mistaken, and in his crudest
errors some truth is always to be found. Every particular truth
being a part of general truth, a fragment of the gospel presents
itself in its proportion as did the gospel itself. The poet who,
uninterested in vice, tells the truth speaks unconsciously and
unwillingly as a Christian, for every moral truth is a part of
Christianity. Christianity, on the other hand, ought to claim
and adopt everything that is true and good. Thereby the *Faust*
of Goethe is a Christian work; and *The Misanthrope* of Molière
is a sermon on the seventeenth verse of the third chapter of The
Letter of James: "The wisdom that is from above is first pure,
then peaceable, gentle, and easy to be entreated, full of mercy
and good fruits, without partiality, and without hypocrisy."

On the other hand, Vinet has this conviction, that private life
and public society, laws and mores, literature and arts—everything should become Christian under the influence of Christianity. True Christianity converts all things into its own substance,
so that everything becomes religion and a perfect connection
is established between all the parts of human life. The authentic Christian life loses none of the natural elements of man; it
only gives up superfluities already condemned by the sages of

all times, and preserves more than many austere pagans desired to retain.

The basic principles of Vinet's literary criticism spring from his conviction that a doctrine is true if it is related to and answers the manifold and apparently contradictory needs of human nature. Thus to know man is the beginning of wisdom. Literature is called upon to furnish us this basis because its testimony is the most universal, the most disinterested and authentic. Hence in the hands of Vinet the study of all literature becomes a study of religious psychology. And Vinet judges the evolution of modern life and literature in Europe by the light of the Christian revelation.

II

THE ROMANTIC MOVEMENT

For naturism or naturalism, nature is the first principle of all things, and God is only another name for the universe. But to Vinet the sky does not tell all the glory and holiness of God. The Lord transcends the universe. To the Christian, nature is only an immense parable. And that which the naturist calls fault or weakness, the Christian calls sin. The Christian, however, will accuse neither the institutions nor one social class of an evil for which the whole of society is responsible. He will not blame mankind either, for he is himself a complete copy and summary of humanity. The Christian will rather seek in his own heart the key to the origin and reality of evil. Like Joseph de Maistre, he will say, "I do not know what the heart of a knave is, but I know that of someone who passes for an honest man, and it is frightful!" In contrast with the easygoing optimist who does not see suffering and evil anywhere, Vinet holds these two principles which do not exclude but complement one another: the inviolable justice of God and his ineffable loving-kindness at work for us.

Vinet was, of course, a contemporary of Chateaubriand (1768–1848), the exemplar of Romanticism who understood life as being essentially feeling. In his *Genius of Christianity* (1802), Chateaubriand had demonstrated that which the classical authors of the seventeenth century, out of religious gravity, had not admitted, and that which the philosophers of the eighteenth century, out of hostility for religion, had denied, namely, that Christianity has been a source of artistic inspiration and inward elevation. Yet Vinet was not in sympathy with this great writer. Vinet gave this judgment about Chateaubriand as representative of Romanticism: he takes colors for reasons, his imagination for his conscience; he mixes constantly the question of the beautiful with that of truth; he inebriates himself with the poetry issuing from great memories; for him, religion is nothing but a solemn enchantment of the imagination. For Vinet, as a whole, Romanticism is pure illusion regarding human life: it dreams of a world that does not exist and cannot exist. Christianity is not an exaltation of sentiment, but a spiritual force issuing from the incarnation, the work of Christ and his reconciling man to God. Vinet transcends, goes beyond, the dualism between the rationalism of the former century, which destroyed ancient religion, and the aesthetic needs of the Romanticists, who rebuilt it for sentimental and artistic reasons. Vinet certainly lessens, if he does not solve, the conflict between scientific reasons and religious symbols.

Another contemporary of Vinet was Lamartine (1790–1869), the creator of personal poetry in France, the first great French lyricist, a great master of the elegy. By inspiration, by inner need, Lamartine entered the government. He was one of the most generous men of his century. Yet, in judging him, Vinet was rather severe. To him Lamartine seems more the courtier and admirer of God than his servant. Vinet was suspicious of naturistic mysticism and of Romanticism as a whole. A religion that is based on feeling for the infinite might lead anywhere.

Against Lamartine's theory that man is but an imperceptible part of an immense unity and that the perfecting of man is a collective and eternal work, Vinet affirms the strange dogma of predestination. This dogma, says Vinet, has really never been rejected by the Christian community. The substance of this dogma sets forth the value of each individuality in the sight of God. Each individuality is dear to him, and with his eyes God follows him in life and death. Were there but *one* Christian on earth, the sight of the eternal Lord would be fixed on that man or woman. The important and practical aspect of the doctrine of predestination, Vinet goes on to say, is that it puts the sovereignty of God in sharp focus and emphasizes the universal and unique character of God as author of all things—in contrast to the proud and stubborn personality of man. Human personality is a mere product of the breath of God. Predestination proclaims our condition of absolute dependence on God as the giver of all life. Predestination is a crushing mystery for human reason, yet it is always there; and Vinet holds that it is not incompatible with the fact that God is love and love is the principle of all that God does.

Returning to Lamartine's poetry, for Vinet, religion (as Pascal said about man) depends more on thought than on space and duration. The ideas of infinity, immensity, eternity, and power may be important in religion, yet they are not religion itself. All these ideas or concepts may superabound in the language of a poet, yet true earnestness may be entirely wanting there. His verses may not be truly religious. Even greatness will be absent from them; for, if the greatness of God consists in his being holy, the greatness of man lies in the feeling that he is not holy and yet he aspires to be. The great aim of Christianity is to unite man once more to God, to transform duty into spontaneous sentiment and feeling into duty, to teach man to love what he ought to do, and to do what he ought to love. Man of himself is incapable of recovering this lost harmony; the work of the living and eternal Christ is to reestablish it; the Lord accomplishes the mysterious union of law and feeling.

III

TRUTH AND PERMANENCE

Vinet loved the classical writers. The twofold secret of the power exerted by the work of great geniuses consists in belonging to their time and yet transcending it. Nothing speaks more in favor of classical studies than the fact that they are disliked by radicals of all kinds. Some, the radicals of the moment, imagine that antiquity has nothing to say; others perceive in it the subtle germ of an aristocracy of culture. In point of fact, nothing speaks more in favor of these studies than this double hostility. These prejudices and reproaches prove only that the study of antiquity combines two elements, progress and stability, and consequently satisfies the law of equilibrium. The development of man can only be completed by these two means: culture of his spirit by Christianity, culture of his mind and taste by the study of antiquity. Reading the classics refines men, and intellectual improvement is often the prelude to spiritual improvement. The New Testament was written in Greek; through reading it, true Christians have become Greeks without knowing it. The Old Testament was written in Hebrew; and its influence has made authentic believers somehow also Orientals. Antiquity! How could we desert it? Never before has it been more precious and more necessary!

Genuine art is that which has truth for its object; false art is that which cultivates illusion and falsehood. The false has never been classical. The good in literature is the true. Truth has power and charm. It is perhaps the first of literary talents, but it is also the rarest. Pascal gave up all mannerism and vain ornamentations, replacing them by perfect truthfulness. He was both true and great. The great, the sublime, is always something involuntary and unforeseen. We are not capable of inventing the truth. Truth exists; it presents itself; and there is within us something capable of recognizing it, joining it, and becoming incorporated with it. To make this point clear, Vinet offers this illustration taken from very ancient times and recalling the usage of primordial hospitality. Before parting from a stranger, the father of the family was wont to break a clay seal on which certain characters were impressed, and giving one half to his guest, he kept the other half. After a lapse of years these two fragments, being brought together again, would fit, so to speak, recognize each other, and be a medium of recognition between the two men who held them. By the evidence thus borne to the relations of former days, the two fragments would become the basis of new relations. Thus it is with man's inner being. The lines, the characters there begun, find their divine complement in the truth. Thus our soul does not, properly speaking, discover the truth, but, rather, recognizes it.

The great, the true, is given to us. To begin to think in order to write or because we want to write is to renounce our best thoughts. Yet meditation helps. True meditation, as the word indicates, puts us into the midst of things—*in medias res,* identifies us with them, makes us live with their life. To analyze is not to meditate; for analysis decomposes, whereas meditation surrounds the whole facts submitted to us. Analysis never arrives at intuition, which in certain subjects is actual knowing; this knowledge by intuition is the peculiar privilege of meditation properly so called. Meditation also leads to simplicity. And the simplification of inner existence is, with respect to both spiritual life and happiness, one of the most pressing wants of modern times.

As a general rule, we must start from truth to have any lasting life. Life is a perpetual rebirth. And in this life the light in our darkness, the happiness in our unhappiness, consist in a faith founded on God, in a hope that depends on him, in a love that ascends to him to redescend thence upon mankind and embrace it as a whole.

VIII

The Evangelical Ministry

I

THEORY OF THE MINISTRY

FOR VINET, faith includes the desire to live to the glory of God; and turning to God or conversion is included in such a desire. Even more, this desire is conversion itself. In the absence of proper instruments, the Lord God appears to ask, "Whom shall I send?" and to expect (from everyone who has the requisite ability for the ministry) the reply of the prophet Isaiah, "Here I am; send me!" (Isa. 6:8). Thus responding and turning to God is conversion. The call to be an Evangelical minister is implicitly a conversion to God. The church's ministry therefore is the consecration of certain members of the Christian flock to the administration of worship and to the spiritual care of men.

The art of arts, the science of sciences, is that of directing men. And men are the most changeable of all beings as well as the most difficult to reach. They are always in a hurry. Modern haste is injurious to man. For instance, he reads too much; he reads carelessly, consequently his being is little nourished. It is his heart, above all, that man must learn to read, but he has no time to read the inner volume (which is his very self). The modern world is full of fugitives. Nowadays many a hermit lives in the world and many a man of the world lives in solitude.

The general and prolonged loneliness of modern men is

injurious to true being, just as is too constant intercourse with material things. It is not good also from a religious point of view that man should be alone (Gen. 2:18), but it would be still less good that he should never be so. By dint of mingling with others, modern man loses his individuality; he exchanges his personal character for the general character; he thinks with the minds of others, he ceases to be himself. In mixing with the world, man loses that native form of his being which constitutes his personality. Truth, in addressing him, would seek to get hold of him in vain; and he, who has gradually allowed others to substitute their being for his, would no longer have the wherewithal to feel, to recognize, and to appropriate the truth.

Vinet finds it a remarkable fact, however, and one that shows that all light is not extinguished in man, that, though man is generally determined by questionable motives, he finds it necessary to disguise them. A man dares not mention them to himself, and still less would he dare to allege them to others; above all, he would not risk directly to propose what was evil to assemblies of men, or, to express it more clearly, to set before men the mere gratification of a lust as a motive of action. To influence men and to guide them, therefore, the minister ought to find a motive for them. A motive is what gives to our inner being impulse and power to act.

To solve this problem, Vinet brings in the fact of man's freedom. Man is only to be determined ultimately by his affections. To overcome one passion, another passion must be called up. One affection can only be destroyed by another affection. But affection can only be excited by facts—by facts, that is, which cause the vibration of one of the two chords of every man's inner being: selfishness or love. The liberty of man, which is a relative thing, cannot consist in acting without motives; it must consist in acting from good motives. The minister desires to present to men only good motives, and such he will present to them.

Vinet reduces all the good motives of men, which the minister can use as levers, to these two: moral goodness (or duty) and happiness. Vinet gives first place to moral good (or duty), which he sums up in gratitude to God. Gratefulness to the Lord is the meaning and the summary of the gospel: "Knowest thou not that 'the goodness of God' leadeth thee to conversion [*metanoia*]?" (Rom. 2:4). Gratefulness is, for Vinet, the only evidently unselfish feeling of which human nature is capable. This very fact made gratitude apt to become the fulcrum of our regeneration.

Vinet's reason for mentioning happiness as the second motive for men is that happiness is essential to human nature and a constitutive part of it. Happiness is also the precondition of devotion and self-sacrifice. To give happiness to others, we must first have it ourselves. Happiness therefore occupies a place among our most disinterested and most generous sentiments. Happiness, as a motive of action, moreover, abounds in that revelation in the name of which the pastor speaks: "I have set before you life and death, . . . therefore choose life, that both thou and thy seed may live!"—said the Lord our God (Deut. 30:19). The first word in the public preaching of Jesus, finally, is the word *blessed!* or *happy!* (Matt. 5:3). It may be said that it is the first word of his religion, which is a doctrine of happiness and of salvation as much as of perfection. As the special property of Jesus' religion is to identify happiness with perfection (Matt. 11:29; James 1:25), the two motives, which Vinet had distinguished for the sake of exposition, are but one.

Historically, the minister has generally taken the name of " pastor " or " shepherd." This is right, for the minister is not only to guide men but also to feed them with a word that is not his own. Just as the shepherd feeds his sheep on green grass that the shepherd does not make, so the pastor or minister feeds his flock with words that simply reproduce God's Word, and applies it to the various needs of men through instruction, direction, encouragement, consolation, and inspiration. The minister is simply a steward of the Word of God. Just as Jesus was sent by God, so the minister is sent by Jesus Christ. The pastor comes in the name of Christ to do out of gratitude all that Jesus Christ did out of pure love. The minister therefore ought to be an authority on the pulpit and in his office. Here Vinet means true authority, that which rests wholly on conviction and zeal, and through which (as through a pure and transparent medium) shine humility and charity. The tone of this true authority ought to be welcome to most modern men.

II

THE NATURE OF PREACHING

The conditions and forms of a sermon ought to answer only to the purpose of Christian eloquence. The sermon supposes no particular form. It follows no convention. In spite of his vast scholarship, Vinet does not follow any historical tradition or pattern. Vinet holds that the preacher should speak in the manner that experience and the study of human nature have discovered to be the best for persuading men of every kind of truth. Vinet does not sketch a particular standard pulpit discourse. Each subject, each necessity experienced, each circumstance will give to the sermon the form that it ought to have.

Since not all flocks are the same, the good preacher always keeps present in his mind the kind of audience he has to address as well as his own aim. Each man, each audience, generally has weak points, which the minister must strengthen, or strong fixations, which should be softened so as to establish a happy medium. To those men and women with too strong a faith, the good pastor preaches " work " and the fact that, in all conditions of life, the Lord's Word is our law. But to men and women who conceive the Christian life as mere activity, the minister would preach faith and meditation. His principle and his aim are to establish an equilibrium by presenting the particular thing that his congregation has forgotten either to think or do. The final goal of the minister is to have his people live a harmonious Christianity of light and love.

The principal quality of a good sermon is clearness. Modern times have weakened the idea of this word. "Clearness" formerly meant brightness, splendor, effulgence. Vinet wishes the word to be restored to its original force. Let clearness be brilliant. Yet simplicity also recommends itself by more than one claim to the pulpit orator. Etymologically speaking, simplicity is the contrary of multiplicity. Simplicity is the absence of any fold (Latin *plica*), or pleat (French *pli* or *repli*), or duplicity. Simplicity would exclude even the expression of a second idea when a first is sufficient. Simplicity resembles conciseness; but conciseness is a sparing of words, while simplicity is the economy of means. Simplicity makes thought take the most direct road to the object. Simplicity does not exclude shades or richness of expression. Just as clearness adorns profound thoughts, simplicity adorns great thoughts; and all the thoughts that the preacher is charged to transmit are great.

But all this being well understood, Vinet wishes us neither to forget nor to suffer it to be forgotten that we have a written religion in the Scriptures, and that God himself has condescended to give a form to its truth. Hence the expressions that come from the minister's mouth ought to have a character of authority that no other word can have. It is thought that elevates speech. The minister's text for preaching is drawn from the Word of God (the Bible) only when the pastor gives it the sense that the text has in the intention of the sacred author. Hence the study and exposition of Scripture (or exegesis) is useless without some knowledge of its ancient languages (or philology).

As a whole, Vinet grants that the boldness and the freedom of the prophets of Israel are not sufficiently felt in modern sermons. A deeper sense of the suffering of humanity, a greater sense of responsibility, a more lively compassion for men, and finally a higher idea of the minister's calling and position ought to place him above vain considerations and notions of propriety with which, in truth, the ministry has nothing to do. That this is not the current idea of the ministry, Vinet grants; but should the minister conform to common notions or should he do his best to reform them? If the maxims of the world about preachers are the measure of the minister's liberty, there is no reason according to society why he should not descend still lower in complaisance to current ideas; if, on the contrary, the minister claims for himself all the liberty awarded to him by Biblical principles, and exercises courage, he shall find that as he fears less, there will be less to fear. If, rather than allow their ministry to be encroached upon, ministers vindicate for it all the authority that belongs to it, there is every reason to believe that the congregations, though surprised at first, will consent and get used to bolder pastors. After all, the world loves courage; it is strong only against the weak. The timidity of ministers causes the boldness of others. Everywhere and on all occasions, provided he follows truth with charity, the ministry of a man will be that which he shall desire it to be. But, accepted or not accepted, it is essential that the minister be what he ought to be.

If the minister speaks in the name of God, he wishes to know nothing but what he has learned from God himself. The principle of the minister's authority is submission to the greater authority of the Word of God. The minister of the gospel announces the gospel. He has to relate not his own private history but the wonders of God. In point of fact, it is God who preaches, and man is but his instrument.

III

THE MINISTER'S FAITH AND DOUBTS

The minister must pursue his work as pastor in the very midst of conflicts between faith and doubt (which Vinet called, in German, *Anfechtungen*) perhaps more frequent and more profound than those of lay people. Whosoever has faith will inevitably have doubts. Doubt is fear of being mistaken and is often a precaution against error. In such a case, to doubt is really to believe in the truth. Proofs, on the other hand, are generally present to the mind, but the inner man at times is not convinced. Antitheses and conflicts are part of Christianity. Conflicts are constant. Despair by itself does not make us Christians. Yet despair may open ways to the truth. Christianity has been favorable to antithesis; and we may say that it is itself full of it. In order to reconcile opposites and oppositions, it is necessary first of all to bring them out. This explains the difference that we may notice between pre-Christian and Christian writers with respect to the use of antithesis. Paganism has suppressed contrasts, so to speak, that it might give a certain unity to life—a factitious unity, no doubt, which consisted in the negation or ignorance of one of the terms of those great antitheses presented by human life. By bringing out clearly those contrasts which it would reconcile and transcend, Christianity has brought to light the antitheses of our existence.

Vinet compares the truth of Christianity to the atmosphere composed of several elements, any one of which, if inhaled alone, would kill us, but, when combined, make possible and support life itself. To begin with, as in Calvin's *Institutes* (I. i. 1), a twofold knowledge (that of God and that of man) is ever present to Vinet. And as in Pascal, God in his divine nature and man in his human nature are continually considered with reference to the other. The glory of the gospel is not only to have made truth divine but to have made it human. The union in Jesus Christ of all the fullness of the Godhood with the fullness of manhood was the program, symbol, support, and substance of a new religion. This unity without confusion, consummated at once in idea and in fact, was the *fiat lux* (Gen. 1:3) of a new genesis, the organization of a second chaos, that is, of our world, which is without form and void.

And Vinet well observes that the two elements, the human and the divine, are not the terms of a contradiction or antinomy in this new religion but the two hemispheres or, if one prefers, the two poles of the truth. Man carries within himself the twofold need of giving himself wholly to God and of remaining wholly human. The religion that does not give all to God is not worthy of the name of religion. On the other hand, a religion mutilating man (while professing to restore him to God) and hence not offering the whole man to God, is not divine because it is not human. True religion is a relation. Suppressing one of the two terms destroys the relation, no matter which of the two terms is suppressed: either God does not exist for man or man does not exist for God. Religion supposes God in the fullness of his Godhead, man in the fullness of his humanhood—two beings, two persons, not merely two names. All the deviations or heresies that have sprung up in Christianity, as well as all the systems conceived outside of Christianity, result in lessening man or in lessening God.

As for Jesus Christ, he is God and man; and it is the same with his teaching. Christianity is drawn at once from the depth of God and from the depth of man. By its two extremities it touches the mysteries of the divine Being and the mysteries of human nature. Without denying the duality of the terms, genuine Christian thought ever seeks to determine the relation between them and to do justice to both of them.

Without doubt, it is God who converts; this is the *principle*. But he converts man by the means of man; this is the *fact*. Vinet means man personal, living, moral. Man is the medium through which God has purposed that truth should come to man. Truth alone is luminous, the medium is only transparent; but let it be truly transparent, and, as far as depends upon us, let not the rays of truth be obscured and broken by an unfaithful medium.

IV

WHAT THE CHURCH IS

According to Vinet, we are not Christians because we have been enrolled in a church or registered in a Christian community. It is not to Christendom that men must go, but to Christ, because the influence of Christianity is due to the immediate contact of Christ with men. Nevertheless, we Christians should not forget that body and that reality which is the church. To make this point clear at a time when men used to take long walks in the country, Vinet offered the following illustration. When, in the noontide of a burning day, our strength and even our life seem to fail through the pains of thirst, we come upon a river, a drop perhaps from its waters restores and revives us, we bless that drop of water; it is that which has refreshed us, not the river; we have not drunk the river, and yet is it not the river that brought us that saving drop? Could we have drunk it but for the river? That mass of water which we have not drunk was needed to bring us the draught which we might drink; thus, all things considered, it is the river that has saved us.

In like manner, in a spiritual sense, it is the church that saves us because it brings us Jesus Christ. The church, that is to say, the Christian community in the succession of centuries, is the stream that brings down to us the name and knowledge of Jesus Christ, and, so to speak, Jesus Christ himself. Without the church, no Christianity and no Christians!

The succession of holy lives in the history of mankind is the tradition of God. These lives are Christianity itself, for Christianity, although it be written in a book, is nevertheless essentially neither a book nor a doctrine, but life gushing eternally from the very heart of God. This life, perpetuated from believer to believer, is a revelation, the tradition of God, a divine testimony. The church therefore is not only a fruit, but an organ of Christianity; it propagates, upholds, and perpetuates Christianity. The church is, properly speaking, the gospel on earth: Jesus Christ among men, the Holy Spirit governing and uniting the faithful.

Christ is still here below, says Vinet; Christ is still contained in mortal flesh. Christ succeeds to himself in the church. The church is a body. Its head (Christ) is in heaven. The church militant has inherited the condition of the humbled and suffering Jesus. Here below, it represents Christ, and will represent him till the end of time. Christ communicates life to the church and determines its actions. The church does nothing of itself, but all through Him—all that he has done while on earth. It carries on his work, by him and for him. The church is the whole body, but it is not the head. While the Master reigns as head in the peace of heaven, the body (which is the church) remains on earth and undergoes all that Jesus Christ would suffer were he still on earth. Having the same spirit, invoking his name, it must needs have the same adversaries, meet the same obstacles, excite the same opposition, and undergo the same suffering. The church must do all this, else it is not the church. The agony of Jesus Christ must continue in the body of the church, or there is no church.

This is what still remains behind the afflictions of Christ; this is the sign that his work is being carried on upon earth; this is the burning yet glorious seal that the Master impresses on those who are his; this is the method by which the church may correspond with its head till the end. Let us not attribute to the body (the church) anything that belongs exclusively to the head; let us not impute to the afflictions of the body the redeeming merit and virtue that belong only to the sufferings of the head; let the body that is the church enter into a community of love and suffering with the head, which is Jesus Christ.

The church is preeminently a spiritual society. "I believe" and "I am" are, on the part of the church, two inseparable affirmations. Every church that does not declare its faith has none. The church is a spiritual work whose glory, condition, and very essence is to continue spiritual. For Vinet, therefore, a church conformed to society, identified with the natural ways of the community, is pure heresy—the only heresy. For Christianity is the choice that we should constantly make between the visible and the invisible things, but if we see no difference, there is no choice, and when there is no choice, there is no church, no Christianity, no religion. In the same way as the human body (when placed in a temperature exactly the same as its own) feels no particular sensation, receives no impression (either good or bad), so it is with the church whose religion is identical with its surroundings. When the church is not different from society, it leaves man as it finds him, and he in his turn leaves the church as he has found it; the reciprocal action is null because the agreement is perfect.

Church and state are two different institutions as to their

spirit and procedure. They should be distinguished with care to avoid pernicious alliances or combinations. The domain of the state is the exercise of force, the maintenance of justice, the enforcement of law and external order even by constraint. The domain of the church, on the contrary, is essentially spiritual. It is free choice, persuasion, goodwill, and charity. The glory of Christianity is to rule only by influence and under the form of liberty. As the church is born of a spiritual necessity, it is higher than the state. The church does not need the state, otherwise it would not be self-sufficient. Hence the church demands from the state the liberty to follow its own spirit and method, resting on its own strength and not on that of the world or state or community.

As an earthly organization, the church is an association that has action for its end. Being "Societies of Believers," the churches ought to be administered in their own way. The idea of church as a society must be complemented by the idea of church as a school, because of the necessarily mixed condition of actual church life. As a matter of fact, some church members adhere personally to its constitutions, and practice the Christian life; whereas other members simply adhere outwardly to the church's principles and have no personal convictions. The latter members, however, may be candidates, as it were, of a later personal religion which they may learn from experience with life. The only legitimate discipline can therefore be but external. One should in no way violate man's conscience and encroach upon the right of God over that conscience.

The Christian is directly taught of God; no man has domination over his faith; he himself ought to derive this faith from the study of Scripture and dependence on the Holy Spirit. The church is his society. If it be a school, the schoolmaster is God himself. The true medium of the church is freedom. Liberty is the only pledge of truth, order, and moderation. In this marvelous atmosphere whatever is false ought to correct or to destroy itself. As the church is made up of believers, they ought to administer it. The preachers of the gospel are not the church's only ministers. The gospel has suppressed the priest. There is, in one sense, only one Priest. He is Jesus Christ. In another sense, there are as many priests as there are believers. The clergy therefore is not the church. There is properly no clergy in a truly Evangelical church. It is the whole church that is the clergy—a Greek word meaning the patrimony of Jesus Christ, the property of God.

V

THE MYSTERY OF THE MINISTRY

The minister is a city set upon a hill. He represents Christianity, and most people judge Christianity by him. This may not be altogether right on the part of the people but it is a fact, and it places the highest responsibility on the minister. Taking him as a symbol of Christianity, people also judge him by the Christianity he preaches and practices. The worst of it is that people require contradictory things from their pastor. They expect him to be perfect and yet want him to be like everybody else. Let the minister pick up the challenge and be the most perfect representative of religion as well as of human life.

As representative of God, the minister knows that preaching is the explication of the Word of God, the exposition of Christian truths, and the application of those truths to his assembled flock. As the church is a great school open to everyone, preaching is, of course, public. Preaching is a part of worship. Worship speaks to God while preaching speaks of him. But since it is only when on a higher level that we can speak worthily of God, preaching that is not of the nature of worship is not authentic preaching.

The Fourth Gospel calls Christ the Word, or Reason. The term is important, for the word is reason expressed and reason is the inner word. The gospel is the Word. The church itself is truth thought in common and spoken in common. Preaching is a mystery—a mystery as to its action and its effects, a mystery of reprobation for some persons and salvation for others. With

Saint-Cyran, Vinet is tempted to call preaching almost a sacrament more awful than that of the altar of the Lord's Supper.

As in Saint-Cyran, so in Vinet, the sovereign grace of God is continually adored and, above all, blessed. And never perhaps has human liberty less cause to lament or to be alarmed. There is a mystery in election, since there are elect ones. Yet Jesus Christ died potentially for all men. In him all men have the possibility of being redeemed. There is nothing in the matter that is unfathomable but the love of God. This love has its sole cause in itself; for, at the Last Day the reprobate will find in their reason the justification of the sentence that condemns them, and the elect alone will be astonished at the decree that beatifies them. Grace is not an isolated fact, but a perpetual effusion, a circulation of life between the members—that is to say, created spirits—and the head which is God, the Father of spirits. In the spiritual sense as in the temporal sense, the creature is continually created. The name of this divine life is charity. God communicates his love (*charité*), which is his life. As we become members of God, we become members of one another, but voluntary members, and by an act of will continually renewed. We are neither absorbed in the head nor in the whole; for love is not less the triumph of individuality than the means and the consummation of unity.

The sovereignty of God in this matter is the first point to be recognized. Yet it does not exclude human responsibility. Preaching is an action that is forceful when it is performed with a clear conscience, that is, with uprightness of intention. Preaching is therefore a divine mystery and a human action. The best part of this action is inward, spiritual, anterior to the act of composing the sermon. The discourse simply finishes the work that prayer should begin.

A preaching that excites no contradiction lacks one of the characteristics of truth. In the same way that the human body when situated in a temperature the same as its own receives no impression and feels no sensation, so it is with a man to whom a religion identical with his own disposition is preached.

Such is natural or national religion: it leaves man as it finds him, and man in his turn leaves that religion as he has found it. The agreement is perfect, because the reciprocal reaction is nil. From Paul's words, "My little children of whom I travail in birth again until Christ be formed in you" (Gal. 4:19), it is clear that the object of the minister is not merely to teach people *their* religion as if they already possessed the true religion and it was *theirs* before they had learned it, but to lay in them the foundation and meaning of life. True religion is properly an instruction and an initiation into the sacred mystery of the Christian life.

People expect the minister to represent human life. Vinet urges him to represent it at its best. Vinet intimately knew Latin, Greek, English, German, French, and Italian literature. He had a Christian, Protestant outlook on the whole of modern culture. He was a Christian humanist. As if in a vision, the God, says Vinet, whom the gospel reveals to us seems to advance toward us with these words: "I am man [in Christ] and I think nothing human alien from me"—*Homo sum, humani nihil a me alienum puto.* God comes and communicates himself to us as man. He borrows from the language of men all sorts of terms capable of expressing the inexpressible condescensions of his free love. Following this vision, the minister will be a humanist in the true sense of the word, that is, an accomplished man. The business of us all is not merely to do well, but to do better; and we really do well only when we seek to do better. Through self-culture and reading the humane classics, the minister also shall end by saying, "I am a man and everything human concerns me"—*"Homo sum. . . ."* The minister will become so in reality. Nothing is so human as Christianity. No one is man so much as the Christian. This is indeed, as the nature of Evangelical preaching requires him to be, a man whom men shall understand.

Pastoral work has this threefold purpose: to promote (1) the material, (2) the moral, and (3) the spiritual interest of the parish by applying to society the Christian spirit and charity.

The Sovereign Pastor cared for the helpless, and gave as a principal characteristic of his church compassion for the unfortunate and care to restore equality by charity. And charity has sometimes rudeness for its true expression. Gentleness is sometimes treachery. We may exercise charity in vehemence and indignation. The fact is that love of good implies hatred of evil. Did not the prophets, the apostles, and Jesus himself freely express wrath?

It is impossible to love good without hating evil; but it is very possible and even too common to hate evil without loving good. This hatred separated from love has not the characteristic of that "perfect hatred" which the royal prophet had vowed against the opponents of his God (Jer. 2:19; Prov. 1:31).

For Vinet, truth consists in feeling as well as in thoughts; the love of good implies the hatred of evil. Love is truth; truth is love; truth is therefore also hatred; and even anger when necessary. But, "O Lord, give us to love as thou lovest, to hate as thou hatest, and to correct as thou correctest!" It is difficult, Vinet grants, to venture, to risk to stand alone at times in one's convictions and actions; but for Vinet, this is the condition, the glory, and the peril of the Christian.

IX

Conclusion: Extraordinary Christianity

I

VINET AND KIERKEGAARD

WHAT WILL HAVE, no doubt, struck our reader is the fact that Vinet is modern, or, even more, contemporary. His words seem to have been written for the crisis of our day.

Because of the present importance of Kierkegaard, we must note that Vinet did not read Kierkegaard, but Kierkegaard read Vinet and wrote in his *Journal*, "Vinet says it in a masterly fashion: 'the teaching of Christianity marks the downfall of the human race and the resurrection of the individual.' "

The purpose of our pages was neither to give a description of contemporary existentialism nor to draw a detailed parallelism of related ideas. But we cannot help pointing out a central concept and a few essentials, letting other students (if they so wish) carry on and complete an investigation of their own.

According to P. H. Tisseau, the following words of Kierkegaard sum up his entire theory of existentialism: "For Christianity, truth does not consist in knowing the truth but in being in the truth. . . . We truly know the truth only when truth becomes life in us. Christ compared truth to a food (John 6:48 ff.) and its assimilation to the act of nourishment. One can see, therefore, the monstrous and unsurpassed distortion of those who make Christianity the object of a learned doctrine

. . . and make truth a knowing, while for primitive Christianity the whole truth was rather a being." But such a central concept of Kierkegaard was asserted by Vinet especially when he said that "to be in the truth is to become, by our affections and our conduct, like Jesus Christ; it is to follow him spiritually in all the events through which he has passed, in his death by our death to sin, in his resurrection by our regeneration, in his invisible glory by our life hid with him in God; in a word, it is spiritually to relive the entire life of Jesus Christ. This only can be called knowing the truth, living in the truth."

Our reader will also remember these words of Kierkegaard: "We should not confuse the Truth with truths. . . . Christ says, 'I am the Truth, the Way, and the Life.' When the Truth itself is the Way, the Way cannot be shortened or suppressed." "Modern confusion has suppressed Christ." "Jesus may still have admirers, but how many imitators? What is the difference," asks Kierkegaard, "between an admirer and an imitator?" And he answers: "An imitator is or strives to be that which he admires, while an admirer remains personally foreign to the object of his admiration. Consciously or not, the admirer does not discover that the object of his admiration (in our case) requires that the admirer should be or strive to be that which he admires." "Only the imitator is the true Christian." These and similar concepts were anticipated by Vinet when he said, for instance, "Christ does not say, 'I show the way . . .' He says, 'I am the way, the truth, and the life.'" The quality of disciples of Jesus Christ is to be an imitator: one is a disciple only at this cost. There are not only lessons, there are examples that he left us to the end that we follow in his tracks.

The space and time allowed to us do not permit us to draw further parallels. It is enough to say that Kierkegaard's dialectics, use of paradox, and affirmations that Christianity is discipleship and solitary foolishness in this world, were anticipated by Vinet. Not only so, but Vinet is brilliant, luminous, crystal-clear, and, by his critique of literature and modern civilization, offers a more comprehensive thought than Kierkegaard.

II

CATHOLICISM AND PROTESTANTISM

It was impossible for Vinet not to admire the sequence and connection of ideas in Catholicism. Catholicism is a historical and moral fact. It derives its force from facts. Catholicism is, in some respects, the Christianity of the natural man. It has for an author man himself, or, rather, human nature. Sublime or popular at will, Catholicism makes itself "all things to all men" in a way that would have surprised Paul, who had adopted these words for his own motto.

It is one of the forces of Catholicism to have translated all its ideas into institutions; each drop of water has been crystallized; the Catholic religion has taken up its position at all points of human life, as has the naval power of England at the entrance of all seas; each important moment or circumstance of a Catholic life has its rite; the holy banner floats everywhere; the Catholic religion is tangible, sensible; it has a body, a form, a color. Protestantism by comparison looks poor: it has for its body bare temples, simple services, cold for cold souls, the roof of the parsonage, and a few inner recollections. Yet Protestantism was once a great force. Protestants should be led to appreciate the Reformation.

Three centuries after Luther, there are still some Protestants who persist in imagining that free inquiry was the essence of Protestantism. These men mistake one of the conditions of life for the life itself, and take the atmosphere for the globe it surrounds. Placing himself back in Reformation times, Vinet sees that in the sixteenth century a reaction against medieval Catholicism takes two forms: the one irreligious (the Renaissance), which at once leaps to atheism; the other religious (Protestantism), which is the Reformation; this last being equally opposed both to Catholicism and to unbelief. Without the latter of these two reactions, what would have become of Christianity? and consequently, what would have become of Catholicism itself?

Protestantism caused Catholicism to reform itself. The Reformation has been the saving of Christianity; without it, not only would Catholicism have failed to purify itself, but it would have known no arrest in its degeneration. Not only is it to the Reformation that the seventeenth century owes great Catholic men such as Bossuet, Fénelon, Pascal, but were it not for Protestantism, Catholicism would no longer exist, because all the branches would have had to perish with the trunk. Rome contends that there would no longer be Christians if there were no longer Catholics; yet but for the Reformation there would no longer be Catholics, because there would no longer be Christians. In saving the trunk, the Reformation has saved the branch; but henceforth it is up to the branch to save itself.

Protestants ought to see that the Reformation was religious, in the most exalted and complete sense of the word; religious, not only through its theological opposition to the religion of the day but by its opposition to unbelief, each day more proud and more aggressive. Protestantism proclaimed salvation through faith; that is to say, the restoration of man solely by his adhesion to the merciful overtures of God. The Reformation found anew an authority higher than that which ruled the nations. Protestantism of the early days might have been only negative, but it made itself positive; might have been only liberty, but became religion.

In ancient times, dogma and morals were a whole, one religious unit, but nearing the sixteenth century, dogma and morals became separated. To believe and to act became two distinct and independent things, each going its own way. Thus disconnected, dogma was but a cipher without key or explanation, while ethics became a mere law without sanction. Two roads were thus open: either to reestablish the broken unity of dogma and morals or to make their division definitive. The Reformers took the first way and reunited belief and conduct; the freethinkers chose the second way and made the divorce of religion and ethics permanent. Addressing itself to the principle of action in man, the Reformation was an action. It occupied itself with ideas only in their relation to life. The Protestantism of Luther and Calvin did not merely make room for religion or irreligion, as some men suppose; but in truth Protestantism was at its birth better than a reformation; it was a restoration. It is so. Potentially it ever will be so.

An attentive examination of documents, says Vinet, would show to an historian unabsorbed by political theories that the powerful impulse of the Reformation sprang from the depths of the inner man. The Reformation subsequently became Protestantism; but originally, it was simply re-formation. Human passions have classed a mystic fact in the order of political facts. The Reformers have been made anti-Catholics in spite of themselves; the word Protestant has become synonymous with anti-Catholic; but in the beginning the cause was spiritual and free from party spirit. Even now the true Protestant is not anti-Catholic; nor the true Catholic anti-Protestant; they are both of Christ if they love Christ; and the superficial divisions that man has traced on the surface are lost in a profound unity the farther we penetrate into the inner life of Christian men.

Vinet is not fond of the current notion that Protestantism has succeeded to Catholicism. He would not have the fifteen centuries that preceded the Reformation proclaimed, in its name, null and void. What existed during those fifteen centuries, and was not interrupted by Protestantism, was the Christian church, which belongs to us, says Vinet, and to which we Protestants belong insofar as we are Christians. Tradition is the treasure of religious thought, amassed by ages, upon the platform of God's positive revelation. We revere the tradition of truth; we only reject that of error. Christianity in this sense is a perpetual fact, a life of humanity, a free and living force. It dates farther back than Calvin. It embraces a horizon more vast than that of the Reformation. Jerome and Augustine in ancient times, Bernard in the Middle Ages, and the Abbot of Saint-Cyran in modern days form part of our tradition.

It is hardly necessary to note that Vinet abounds in fertile ideas and sharp contrasts, and in presenting his vast thought, the present writer is not responsible for every one of his statements—especially when taken in isolation. Yet, Vinet would say that every complete truth has two sides, particularly in religion; for religion is essentially the mediatrix that leads all the dualities of human existence back to unity. Every truth is composed of two truths united by a mystery; the abuse of one produced the abuse of the other. Catholicism and Protestantism, considered as half-truths, mutually occasion and beget one another; and thus it is that the dogmas of the two communions should have been formally fought by pious Catholic and Protestant men. It was already so in the earliest days of Christianity. Each of the two earliest churches had its watchword: that of the Jewish church was *law,* and that of the Christian church was *faith.* The error of the Jews lay in reducing everything to works, and not rising up to faith; the error of the Christians consisted in failing to see that the true faith is a work, and that, if faith be not action, it is nothing. Now, these two errors do not so much characterize two epochs in succession as two classes or kinds of persons or two tendencies that continually reproduce themselves at all times and in all places.

As our reader has undoubtedly noticed, Vinet's writings (like Augustine's) abound in antitheses and contradictions. The key to their solution, that is, to our understanding his opposite statements, was given by Vinet himself. To understand a statement, we must keep present the situation, the audience, the men to whom the words are addressed, and the purpose of their author. Vinet would write one thing for readers in Paris and say another thing—even the opposite—to an audience in Basel or in Lausanne. Words are forces to be applied according to the concrete situations. Vinet's purpose is to move the reader of any party into a transcendent medium. In each man and in each audience there is indeed always a weak side to be strengthened, or a strong point to be weakened so as to establish a happy medium or equilibrium. To those in whom faith prevails, Vinet would recommend *works,* insisting that whatever change may have taken place in our status before God, his law remains the law. But to those who emphasize virtue and salvation by works, Vinet would preach *faith* and demand the surrender of merely human virtues. The principle of Vinet is the same as that of Augustine, that is to say, to keep the whole truth in balance by overemphasizing and inculcating the particular truth that men had forgotten either to believe or to practice. Vinet's final aim is to have us reach that luminous Christianity which was his. It is not without reason that, in the twentieth century, in Paris and Buenos Aires, Vinet was called the Augustine of Protestantism.

III

SOMETHING BEYOND

For Vinet, human society shall be living and fair only in the measure in which an even greater number of men will have accepted and reconciled within themselves order and liberty. Yet it ought not to be believed that these two principles (order and freedom) can automatically cooperate by themselves. We need a third principle that would harmonize the two by its sway over them. We must find and love something that includes the two and is their transcendent and living unity.

This third superior principle, this unifying and transforming force, is Christianity as understood by Vinet. To him, Christianity is the only possible seed of freedom and progress. Liberty, order, and Christianity are three inseparable correlatives. Vinet realizes the fact that waving such a banner indisposes two opposite camps: the party of those who wish to extirpate Christianity so as to save human liberty and progress, and the party of those who wish to chain liberty and social progress so as to save their brand of Christianity. Vinet understands such opponents and consequently fears them not. Vinet grants that the alliance of churches and despotism has, since the French Revolution, brought Christianity under suspicion and caused the enmity of many (if not all) progressive minds in the world. Yet Vinet does not lose heart and hopes for better days. He strives to convince the two parties mentioned above that neither will ever triumph over the other. He reminds the liberals and radicals that wherever the divine ray of light has not arrived, liberalism is only an affair of pride and logic; as long as the liberalism of the masses is not rooted in genuine Christianity, democracy shall be a mere confederation of selfish interests, a stepping back into barbarism and savagery; it will not only be a sterile theory but the ruin of mankind. To those radicals and socialists who charge Christianity with being mere apathetic resignation, Vinet says: "Those who think so have not yet understood Christianity. Like every axis, the Christian religion has two opposite poles: submission and liberty, ardor and patience, the present and the future, the visible and the invisible, the ideal and the practical, heaven and earth."

To certain self-styled Christians, on the other hand, Vinet did point out the fact that they had hardly considered the appalling social problems of those days, the industrial exploitation of simpleminded people, and the increasing poverty of the masses. Such a kind of supposed Christianity had not only intensified the suffering of men but even justified the gravest abuses. Vinet perceived the lack of charity in Protestants of his time, their emphasis on law and order, their forgetting that, as justice is to charity what the trunk of a tree is to the root, there can be no true justice where the love of God and to God is absent.

From the whole of Vinet's life and thought it is clear that he was not a professional preacher who, in an already tense world and aggressive modern society, urged men to exercise faith and more faith. Such an emphasis would still increase tensions, and toward what, no one really knows. When Mussolini and Hitler demanded faith, faith in their system, had not such a faith without love already brought us to the edge of the abyss? Vinet knew other human factors besides mere faith, and further values drawn from the history of man. Vinet would rather recommend meditation, contemplation, serenity, social understanding, and charity in all human relations. He knew that the earliest Christian church was not a theological society in which each member, Bible in hand, was telling others what to believe and to do. Vinet knew better. The early church was, rather, a society of mutual assistance born of a new love.

While meditating on Acts 4:34, Vinet noted that, if communism as practiced among the early Christians is not to be taken as an external rule for us today, the fact, however, shows that once the gospel had social effects and certainly is for modern men a lesson in charity. Let there be no doubt: the purpose of the gospel is to create charity in men. The gospel has a social content and bearing. According to the early Christian records, for example, in The Gospel of Matthew (ch. 25:31–40), Jesus identified himself with suffering humanity; and the last words of his ministry were an announcement of men's judgment according to their charitable action among men. According to Paul (I Tim. 1:5) and John (I John 4:16), the purpose of God's revelation and law is to create charity in men, and such a love has been, is, and ever will be greater than faith (I Cor. 13:13). On this point some Protestants too need conversion. Conversion implies a general sacrifice without reservation and regret, expecting henceforth from God no other reward except God himself. Charity casts out fear: anxiety for one's own personal salvation is transposed on the higher plane of anxiety for other men. Personal anxiety is thus transformed into charity, into caring, into a new love for men out of love for God. Charity is full of devotion, of hope, of happiness. True conversion to God involves an earnest surrender of man's virtues—even more than of his vices. Salvation is from God, grasped by faith, through the cross on which his Son reveals man both as man is and should be. Conversion implies so complete an abjuration of all the natural principles of man that it could not be attributed to human precept and example. These, however excellent they might be, could not produce in us so thorough a revolution as a new love for God and men. Vinet

felt indeed that one cannot, except by loving God with a
sovereign love, accept either life or death and that to love God
is to have discovered the secret of life.

To Vinet as a Christian must be ascribed the wonderful
vitality and broadness of his work. The secret of his achievement
was simple: Vinet did not rest upon the authority of the communities around him, just repeating what everybody feels and
knows; Vinet dared to remain faithful to the inner testimony
of the Living Christ, and expressed what that Eternal Spirit
would say about our modern society and world. Vinet's personality and thought, his role and influence, organically pro-
ceeded from his personal Christianity. He commented from a
Christian point of view on practically the whole of French
literature. Vinet is one of the best historians of French and
related thought. His insight into the nature of modern life
and civilization was truly prophetic. Vinet's Christianity was
not a mere Sunday-morning affair but a matter of his everyday
life and constant thought. He did not go to church for one
hour a week, then back to business as usual. The reason is that
he had *a Christian and Protestant outlook* not only about a
church building but *about all things*—about the society, politics, science, art, literature, civilization, and culture of our age.
Such a vast outlook and comprehension make Vinet what he is,
that is, the creator of a truly modern Christian humanism.

Noting that in his age Protestantism had been watered down
to conform to the mores of nations and communities, Vinet at
times was bitter toward commonplace Protestantism and on
the verge of rejecting it, saying that he accepted historical Protestant thought only as a starting point, but that his own personal religion was something beyond. He even stated that
neither Catholicism nor Protestantism as found around him
would have any future, since the world as a whole would
never accept either the Catholicism or the Protestantism that
he knew. For Vinet, Protestantism is not religion, but the starting point of religion. It is the principle of liberty and individuality applied to religious matters. It is consequently not from

Protestantism that Vinet demands unity; this would be a contradiction in terms. Ceaselessly making use of the right of free interpretation of the Bible, Protestants divide and subdivide on account of a single word or even a syllable; they incessantly formulate and lose (in their search after doctrinal or disciplinary precision) the best of their thought and substance. Yet Vinet hopes that this waste of time and energy may be only apparent. For him, rejection of dogmas after all is better than servile acceptance of tenets with which we have nothing in common, unless we are united to them in our inner self.

If Vinet once called both the Catholics and Protestants of his time "nothing more than the empty forms of once living beings," yet he hopes that the world would still belong to a Christianity that would be the true Catholicism and the true Protestantism of humanity, to a Christianity that would be at once liberty and unity. Unity for Vinet is in the present Kingdom of Jesus Christ and in the Spirit. This spiritual power, this bond of faith and love, prepares that sacred federation wherein renewed men and women lose their superficial denominations to be all alike the heralds of rightness, the salt of the earth, and the messengers of him who has called us out of darkness into his marvelous light.

IV

Extraordinary Christianity

Man has separated himself from God. The storms of passion, says Vinet, have broken the mysterious cable that held the human vessel in port. Shaken to its base, and feeling itself driven upon unknown seas, the ship seeks to rebind itself to the shore; it endeavors to renew its broken strands; it makes a desperate effort to reestablish those connections without which it can have neither peace nor security. In the midst of his greatest wanderings, man never loses the idea of his origin and destiny; a dim recollection of his ancient harmony pursues and agitates him; and without renouncing his passions, he longs to reattach his being (full of darkness and misery) to something luminous and peaceful, his fleeting life to something immovable and eternal. Yet, though abandoned by man, God has never ceased to love and to seek man. Man has invented many religions of his own. The Lord still offers the religion of God. It alone responds to all the wants of man and offers to each of his faculties an inexhaustible sustenance. Christianity is a religion of the imagination, to which it offers magnificent horizons; a religion of the heart, which it softens by the exhibition of a love above all love; a religion of thought, which it attaches to the contemplation of a vast and harmonious system; a religion of the conscience, which it renders at once delicate and tranquil; but, above all, a religion of the grace and love of God.

In the general history of man, Christianity, if we judge it from a human point of view, is an accident; if we judge it from a Christian point of view, it is a supernatural dispensation. The view of a spontaneous evolution is unable, according to Vinet, to explain the fact which, nineteen centuries ago, potentially created a new world, a new humanity, and changed the starting point of all ideas. It is not mankind which, by the concurrence of its philosophies and combined results of its history, gave birth to Jesus Christ. He is without father, without mother, without ancestry here on earth. He does not continue, he interrupts the course of time. He makes the stream of our thoughts and events to flow in another channel. Not only Jesus Christ, but the whole gospel is extraordinary. In the midst of our general decline, Christianity is the one thing that is ever new, young, and inexhaustible. The church needs a new heroic age. Christianity is the eternal youth of the human race, but it is so only if its followers are extraordinary and live on earth like citizens of heaven.

Vinet boldly predicts that Christianity cannot rise in the world to its due rank and to the influence delegated to it; nay, it cannot even survive except on condition of becoming again extraordinary. Christianity is not to perish because the extraordinary element (which essentially belongs to it) will not perish.

But were it possible that this element could disappear, nothing would prevent Christianity from disappearing too. A church may die of languor in full orthodoxy; and neology threatens it less than theological precision. The worst of all heresies is indifference.

Authentic Christianity has always been, but is now more than ever, in the position of a besieged army that can save itself only by rushing upon its besiegers. In proportion as we fear less, there will be less to fear; but to refuse to battle would be to avow defeat. It is with Christianity as with war. He must be mad who, seeing improvement in the art of attacking, should not place himself (by choice of weapons and skill in using them) on the level with his adversary. If authentic Christianity issues from God, then the religion of God cannot tolerate mediocrity. The mediocre is the false. It is difficult, Vinet allows, to dare to stand alone in one's opinion and conduct; yet it is a sure thing that he is no Christian who is not called upon to do so at one time or the other. Each of us may be called to do so; this is the distinction, the delight, and the risk of the Christian.

All this may sound strange, even impossible. Yet, says Vinet, just as an intrepid French warrior once said that *"impossible"* is not a French word, so with how much more reason may we say that it is not a Christian word. Christians are humanity restored, a race of God. The greatness of God is to be holy, and the greatness of man is to aspire to be so. God is our end and the accomplishment of our destiny. Christianity is not a doctrine; it is a point of view, a starting point from which we see all things, and all things under a new and original aspect. Authentic Christian faith is the victory over the world. The gospel is more than a symbol or part of life; it is the only true life; it is life itself and its realization. Without love for man as man, all our individual affections, whether of family or country, would not raise us above animals. Each of these special affections deserves the name of love only when, having been perfected by the Spirit of God, it has become *charity*.

Hence, while there is still time, let us do good to all men (Gal. 6:10). According to the divine dispensation, there is in the world a loaf for every hungry man, a coat for every naked one, a consolation for each misfortune, a satisfaction for each need. The balance would be exact if men had not disturbed it. It is not God who is to blame. It is ourselves. He has permitted this inequality only in order to allow us to efface, or at all events to mitigate, human suffering. God has willed that we should owe something to one another. He has willed that the reestablishment of the equilibrium should be our work. To be in the truth is not to be a spectator of the truth but to live the life of Jesus Christ. Mankind suffers and groans; we must suffer and work with her; we must pray for her; we must share that travail in birth which convulses and rends her, for it aims at nothing else than bringing a new world to God.

Selected Bibliography in English

As explained in the Introduction the original long list of French editions of Vinet, German translations, Italian, and Spanish selections from his works and foreign books about him as well as our innumerable references and notes had to be omitted. If a reader wants to verify statements or pursue a study of Vinet, he may find a copy of the original typescript (with lengthy foreign bibliography, innumerable references, and notes) in the libraries of Columbia Theological Seminary in Decatur, Georgia, of Union Theological Seminary in New York City, and of the School (*Faculté*) of Theology of the University of Geneva. We list here works of Vinet or about him in English as well as a few indispensable books and articles on the Reformed tradition which Vinet reexpressed in his own terms and in the new situation of his day.

Bucer, Martin, *Instruction in Christian Love* (1523), tr. by Paul T. Fuhrmann. John Knox Press, 1952.

Calvin, John, *Instruction in Faith*(1537), tr. and ed. by Paul T. Fuhrmann. The Westminster Press, 1949.

Erskine, Thomas, *Remarks on the Internal Evidence for the Truth of Revealed Religion,* 2d American edition from the 5th Edinburgh edition. A. Finley, 1823.

Frommel, Gaston, *The Psychology of Christian Faith, being selections from the writings of the late G. Frommel,* tr. from the French by J. M. Wilson and ed. with Introduction by J. V. Bartlet. London: Student Christian Movement Press, Ltd., 1928.

Fuhrmann, Paul T., "Alexander Vinet and His Theology," *The Lutheran Church Quarterly,* Vol. XIX, No. 3, July, 1946, pp. 235–251.

——— *An Introduction to the Great Creeds of the Church.* The Westminster Press, 1960.

———— "Calvin, The Expositor of Scripture," *Interpretation—A Journal of Bible and Theology,* Vol. VI, No. 2, April, 1952, pp. 188–209.

———— "Saint-Cyran, Precursor of Pascal," critical book review in *The Lutheran Church Quarterly,* Vol. XX, No. 4, October, 1948, pp. 390–392.

———— "The Idea of the Imitation of Christ," *The Lutheran Church Quarterly,* Vol. XX, No. 1, January, 1948, pp. 3–10.

———— *The Theology of Conscience in Pascal and His Swiss Protestant Successors.* The Golden Hind Press, 1933.

Henderson, Henry F., *Erskine of Linlathen—Selections and Biography.* Edinburgh and London: O. Anderson & F. Ferrier, 1899.

Lane, Laura M., *The Life and Writings of A. Vinet,* with an Introduction by F. W. Farrar. Edinburgh: T. & T. Clark, 1890.

Lehmann, Paul L., *Forgiveness: Decisive Issue in Protestant Thought,* with a Foreword by Reinhold Niebuhr. Harper & Brothers, 1940.

McNeill, John T., *A History of the Cure of Souls.* Harper & Brothers, 1951.

On Pascal, pp. 215, 291–292; on Saint-Cyran, pp. 303–304; on Vinet, pp. 215, 258, and 326.

———— *The History and Character of Calvinism.* Oxford University Press, 1954.

On Vinet, pp. 369, 396, and 417.

Pressensé, Edmond de, *Contemporary Portraits,* tr., by A. H. Holmden. A. D. F. Randolph & Co., 1890.

On Vinet, pp. 231–279.

Sanderman, R. J., "Alexandre Rodophe Vinet," *Evangelical Succession,* pp. 219–254. The title page of the copy of this book consulted (at the Biblical Seminary in New York City and located at LS13EV14) was missing. From types and works referred to, this volume seems to have been published in Edinburgh after 1883.

Schneider, Herbert W., "The Development in Protestantism During the Nineteenth Century," *Journal of World History,* Vol. VI, No. 1, pp. 98–121.

On Vinet, pp. 99–100.

Vinet, Alexander R., *An Essay on the Profession of Personal Religious Conviction, Upon the Separation of Church and State Considered with Reference to the Fulfilment of That Duty,* tr. by Charles T. Jones. London: Jackson & Walford, 1843.

———— *Evangelical Meditations,* tr. by Prof. Edward Masson. Edinburgh: T. & T. Clark, 1858.

———— *Gospel Studies.* Glasgow and London: William Collins, n.d. This anonymous translation was reprinted in the U.S.A. with an Introduction by Robert Baird. M. W. Dodd, 1849.

———— *History of French Literature in the Eighteenth Century,* tr. by James Bryce. Edinburgh: T. & T. Clark, 1854.

———— *Homiletics; or, The Theory of Preaching,* tr. and ed. by A. R. Fausset. Edinburgh: T. & T. Clark, 1858.

———— *Homiletics; or, The Theory of Preaching,* tr. and ed. by Thomas H. Skinner. S. C. Griggs, 2d ed., 1854.

———— *Montaigne; The Endless Study and Other Miscellanies,* tr. with Introduction and Notes by Robert Turnbull. M. W. Dodd, 1850.

———— *Outlines of Philosophy and Literature.* London: Alexander Strahan, 1865.

———— *Outlines of Theology.* London: Alexander Strahan, 1866.

———— *Pastoral Theology; or, The Theory of the Evangelical Ministry,* tr. and ed. by Thomas H. Skinner. Harper & Brothers, 1853. A Scottish translation was published by T. & T. Clark of Edinburgh.

———— *Studies on Pascal,* tr. by Thomas Smith. Edinburgh: T. & T. Clark, 1859.

———— *Vital Christianity—Essays and Discourses on the Religion of Man and the Religion of God,* tr. by Robert Turnbull. Edinburgh: T. & T. Clark, 1846.